The POPEYE and Friends Knitting Book

The Popeye and Friends Knitting Book

Melinda Coss

ST. MARTIN'S PRESS

The author would like to thank Suzanne Dosell for
being her right arm and Eleanor Sigmeou, a great
young designer of the future.

The Popeye and Friends Knitting Book

Copyright © 1989 by King Features Syndicate, Inc.

Copyright © 1989 by King Features Syndicate, Inc./Fleischer Studios, Inc.

Copyright © 1989 by King Features Entertainment, Inc./King Features Syndicate, Inc.

For information, address
St Martin's Press, 175 Fifth Avenue, New York, N.Y. 10010.

Library of Congress Cataloging-in-Publication Data
Coss, Melinda.
   The popeye and friends knitting book/Melinda Coss
      p. cm.
   1. Knitting—Patterns. 2. Cartoon characters. I. Title.
TT825.C717 1989   746.9'2—dc19   89-4052

ISBN 0-312-02052-X

First U.S. edition

Typeset by Scribes, Exeter, Devon

Printed in Portugal by
Printer Portuguesa

10 9 8 7 6 5 4 3 2 1

Produced by the Justin Knowles Publishing Group,
9 Colleton Crescent, Exeter EX2 4BY, UK.

Contents

Techniques

Reading the Charts

Explanatory charts show the color designs with stitch symbols added where necessary. Each square represents one stitch across, i.e., horizontally, and one row up, i.e., vertically. Use the charts in conjunction with the written instructions, which will tell you where and when to incorporate them. Any colors required or symbols used will be explained in the pattern. Always assume that you are working in stockinette stitch unless otherwise instructed.

If you are not experienced in the use of charts, remember that when you look at the flat page you are looking at a graphic representation of the right side of your work, i.e., the smooth side of stockinette stitch. For this reason, wherever possible, the charts begin with a right side row so that you can see exactly what is going on as you knit. Knit rows are worked from right to left and purl rows from left to right.

Intarsia

Intarsia is the term used for the technique of color knitting whereby each area of color is worked using a separate ball of yarn, rather than carrying yarns from one area to another as in the fairisle technique. Any design that involves large blocks of isolated color that are not going to be repeated along a row or required again a few rows later, should be worked in this way.

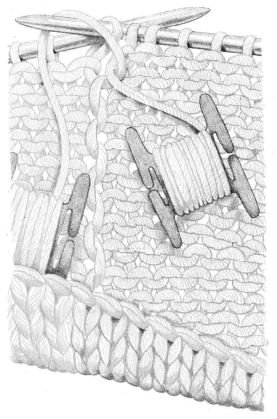

There are no limitations to the number of colors that may be used on any one row, apart from those imposed by lack of patience and/or dexterity. Avoid getting into a tangle with too many separate balls of yarn hanging from the back of the work and remember that every time a new ball of yarn is introduced and broken off after use, two extra ends are produced that will have to be secured at the end of the day. When ends are left, always make sure that they are long enough to thread up so that they may be properly fastened with a pointed tapestry needle. Do this very carefully through the backs of the worked stitches to avoid distorting the design on the right side of the work. The ends that are left should never be knotted because they will make the wrong side of the work look extremely unsightly and they will invariably work themselves loose and create problems at a later stage.

If only a few large, regular areas of color are being worked, avoid tangling the wool by laying the different balls of yarn on a table in front of you or keep them separate in individual jam jars or shoe-boxes. However, this requires careful turning at the end of every row so that the strands do not become twisted.

The easiest method is to use small bobbins that hold each yarn separately and that hang at the back of the work. Such bobbins are available at most large yarn stores or they may be made at home out of stiff card. They come in a variety of shapes, but all have a narrow slit in them that keeps the wound yarn in place but allows the knitter to unwind a controlled amount as and when required. When winding yarn on to a bobbin, try to wind sufficient to complete an entire area of color, but don't overwind, as heavy bobbins may pull stitches out of shape.

When you change color from one stitch to another, it is essential that you twist the yarns around one another before dropping the old color and working the first stitch in the new color. This prevents a hole from forming. If it is not done, there is no strand to connect the last stitch worked in color

When you use the intarsia method, twist the yarns firmly together when you change colors.

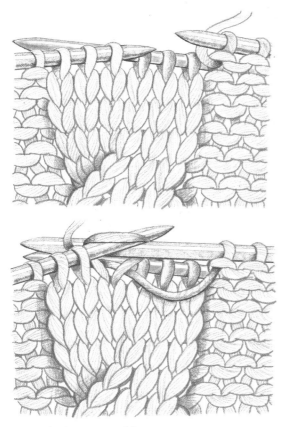

The front cross cable.

"A" to the first stitch worked in color "B". This twisting should also be done quite firmly to prevent a gap from appearing after the work has settled.

Cables

A basic cable is simply a twist in the knitted fabric caused by working a small number of stitches out of sequence every few rows. This is done by slipping the stitches on to a needle and leaving them at the front or the back of the work while the next stitches on the left-hand needle are worked. The held stitches are then worked normally.

Making a Bobble

There are numerous variations on the theme of bobble making, but in this book we have used just one, abbreviated as MB. If worked on a right side row, the bobble will hang on the right side, if worked on a wrong side row, push it through to the right side.

1. When the MB position on the row has been reached, make 5 stitches out of the next one by knitting into its front, then its back, front, back and front again before slipping it off the LH needle.
2. Turn the work and knit these 5 stitches only.
3. Turn the work, purl 5 and repeat the last 2 rows.
4. Using the point of the left-hand needle, lift the bobble stitches, in order, over the first one on the right-hand needle, i.e., 2nd, 3rd, 4th and 5th, so that one stitch remains.

After completing the bobble, the work may continue as normal, the single stitch having been restored to its original position on the row.

Seams

The final sewing up of your knitting can make or break a garment, however carefully it may have been knitted. This is why the making up instructions after every set of knitting instructions should be followed exactly, especially to the type of seam to be used and the order in which the seams are to be worked.

Before starting any piece of work, always leave an end of yarn long enough to complete a substantial section, if not the whole length, of the eventual seam. After working a couple of rows, wind this up and pin it to the work to keep it out of the way. If required, also leave a sizeable end when the work has been completed. This saves having to join in new ends that may well work loose, especially at stress points.

The secret of perfect-looking seams is uniformity and regularity of stitch. Two pieces that have been worked in the same stitch should be joined row for row, and all work should be pinned first to ensure an even distribution of fabrics. When joining work that has a design on both pieces, take great care to match the colors, changing the color you are using to sew the seam where necessary.

Backstitch Pin the two pieces of work together, right sides facing, making sure that the edges are absolutely flush. Always leave as narrow a seam allowance as possible to reduce unnecessary bulk. Keep the line of backstitches straight, using the lines of the knitted stitches as a guide. All the stitches should be identical in length, one starting immediately after the previous one has finished. On the side of the work facing you, the stitches should form a continuous, straight line. If the seam is starting at the edge of the work, close the edges with an overcast stitch.

Keep the stitch line straight and by pulling the yarn fairly firmly after each stitch, no gaps should appear when the work is opened out and the seam pulled apart.

This seam is suitable for lightweight yarns or when an untidy selvedge has been worked.

Flat seam This seam is a slight contradiction in terms since it involves an oversewing action, but when the work is opened out it will do so completely and lie quite flat, unlike a backstitched seam.

Use a blunt-ended tapestry needle to avoid splitting the knitted stitches. Pin both pieces right sides together and hold the work as shown. The needle is placed through the very edge stitch on the back piece and then through the very edge stitch on the front piece. The yarn is pulled through and the action repeated, with the needle being placed through exactly the same part of each stitch every time. Always work through the edge stitch only. If you take in more than this, a lumpy, untidy seam that will never lie flat will be produced.

When two pieces of stockinette stitch are to be joined with a flat seam, do not work any special selvedge such as knitting every edge stitch. Just work the edge stitches normally but as tightly as possible, using only the tip of your needle. When you come to work the seam, place the needle behind the knots of the edge stitches and not the looser strands that run between the knots, since these will not provide a firm enough base for the seam, which will appear gappy when opened out.

Flat seams are essential for heavy-weight yarns where a backstitch would create far too much bulk. They should also be used for attaching button-bands, collars and so forth, where flatness and neatness are essential.

Borders, waistbands, cuffs and any other part of a garment where the edge of the seam will be visible should be joined with a flat seam, even if the remainder of the garment is to have a backstitched seam. Start with a flat seam until the rib/border is complete and then change over to a backstitch, taking in a tiny seam allowance at first and then smoothly widening it without making a sudden inroad into the work.

Sewn slip stitch If one piece of work is to be placed on top of another, for example when turning in a double neckband, folding over a hem or attaching the edges of pocket borders, a sewn slip stitch should be used.

When turning in a neckband that has been bound off, the needle should be placed through the bound-off edge and then through the same stitch but on the row where it was initially knitted up. It is essential to follow the line of the stitch in this way to avoid twisting the neckband. By repeating the action, the visible sewn stitch runs at a diagonal.

The same rule applies when sewing down a neckband that has not been bound off but that has had its stitches held on a thread. The only difference is that the needle is placed through the actual held stitch, thus securing it. When each stitch has been slip stitched down, the thread may be removed. This method allows for a neckband with more "give" than one that has been bound off.

On pocket borders, use the line of stitches on the main work as a guide to produce a perfectly straight vertical line of stitches. Place the needle through one strand of the main work stitch and then behind the knot of the border edge stitch, as for a flat seam.

Making a pompon

With the aid of a circular object measuring approximately 4½in across, draw and cut out two cardboard circles. Cut a smaller circle (approximately 1in across) from the center of each piece. Place these two circles together and wind your yarn through the center hole and around the frame. Continue to wind the yarn evenly around the frame until the center hole is almost full. Holding the circles firmly with your left hand, cut through all the yarn

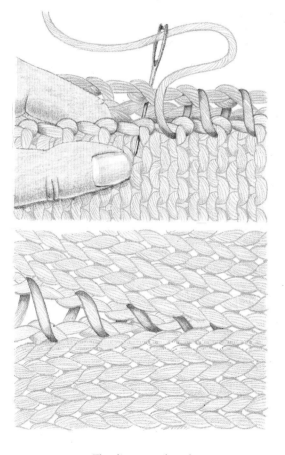

The diagrams show how you should hold the knitting to work a flat seam and how your work will look on the right side.

between the two edges of cardboard. Ease the two pieces of cardboard apart and firmly tie a length of yarn around the middle, leaving a loose end. Pull away the cardboard, gently fan out the yarn and trim. Attach the pompon to your garment by sewing the loose end to your garment.

Gauge

Knitting is the process of making a series of interconnecting loops. Gauge is the term used to describe the actual stitch size – its width regulating the stitch gauge measurement, and its depth regulating the row gauge measurement. Obtaining a particular gauge is not a magical skill, denied to all but the initiated. It is a technicality, the controlling factor of which is the size of needles used by the knitter.

Since all knitting instructions are drafted to size using mathematical calculations that relate to one gauge and one gauge only, you must achieve the stated gauge before you start work or you will have no control over the size of the finished garment.

At the beginning of every pattern a gauge measurement is given, using a specific stitch and needle size – e.g., "using No.8 needles and measured over st st, 18 sts and 24 rows = 4in square". You must work a gauge sample using the same stitch and needle size as quoted. Cast on the appropriate number of stitches plus at least two extra, because edge stitches do not give an accurate measurement. When it is complete, lay the gauge sample or swatch on a flat surface and, taking great care not to squash or stretch it, measure the gauge. If there are too few stitches, your gauge is too loose. Use needles that are one size smaller to work another swatch. If there are too many stitches, your gauge is too tight. Use needles that are one size larger to work another swatch.

Even if you have to change needle sizes several times, *keep working swatches until you get it right*. You save no time by skipping this stage of the work; if you do not get the correct gauge, you risk having to undo an entire garment that has worked out to the wrong size. You may feel that a slight difference is negligible, but a gauge measurement that is only a fraction of a stitch out in every inch will result in the garment being the wrong size, since each fraction will be multiplied by the number of inches across the work.

If you have to change your needle size to achieve the correct gauge for the main stitch, remember to adjust, in ratio, the needles used for other parts of the garment that are worked on different sized needles. For example, if you are using one size smaller needles than are quoted for stockinette stitch, use one size smaller needles than are quoted for the ribs.

Many people worry unnecessarily about row gauge, changing their needle size even though they have achieved the correct stitch gauge. Although important, row gauge does vary considerably from yarn to yarn and from knitter to knitter. If your stitch gauge is absolutely accurate, your row gauge will be only slightly out. Nevertheless, keep an eye on your work, especially when working something like a sleeve that has been calculated in rows rather than inches, and compare it with the measurement chart in case it is noticeably longer or shorter.

The fairisle method of color knitting can make a great deal of difference to your gauge. If you are working a motif in fairisle on a one-color background, take extra care with the gauge, working as loosely as possible so that the motif area does not pull more tightly than the stitches around it, so causing your work to pucker and the actual motif to become distorted. To avoid this, it is advisable to use the intarsia method wherever practicable (*see* page 7).

Dagwood's Jacket

This Fifties-style baseball jacket is Dagwood's pride and joy. Worked in light-weight worsted wool in stockinette stitch, the Jacquard sleeves are simple to work using the fairisle method.

Back

Using No. 4 needles and ecru, cast on 105/109/113/117/121 sts.

Row 1: *k1, p1, rep from * to end.

Row 2: *p1, k1, rep from * to end.

Repeat these 2 rows twice more. Change to black, rib 4 rows, change to ecru, rib 6 rows, inc 12/14/16/18/20 sts evenly across the last row of rib (117/123/129/135/141 sts). Change to No. 6 needles and black and begin following the chart (*see* pages 12–13) in st st to armhole shaping.

Shape raglan: bind off 2 sts at beg of next 2 rows.

Row 3: k3, k2 tog, k to last 5 sts, ssk, k3.

Row 4: purl.

Row 5: k3, k3 tog, k to last 6 sts, sktpo, k3.

Row 6: purl.

Repeat last 4 rows 5/6/7/8/9 times, then repeat 3rd and 4th rows 22/21/20/19/18 times. Bind off remaining 33/35/37/39/41 sts.

Materials

Melinda Coss light-weight worsted – black: 16oz; ecru: 6oz; lilac: 3½oz; pink and yellow: less than 1¾oz of each. A separating zipper measuring 21¾/22/22¾/23¼/24in. If you have trouble finding the right size separating zipper, special zippers can be ordered from Feibusch Zippers, 33 Allen Street, New York, NY 10002; telephone: (212) 226-3964. This store carries nylon separating zippers in all types and styles and in a wide variety of colors for about $5 each. Inquire about price and shipping.

Needles

One pair of No. 4 and one pair of No. 6 needles.

Gauge

Using No. 6 needles and measured over st st, 22 sts and 28 rows = 4in square. Ribs are worked on No. 4 needles.

Incorporate the chart opposite into the back of the jacket, positioning it as described on page 11. The colored lines indicate the area to be worked for each of the five sizes. Charts 2 and 3 should be incorporated into the right front, while chart 3 should be incorporated into the left front (*see* page 14).

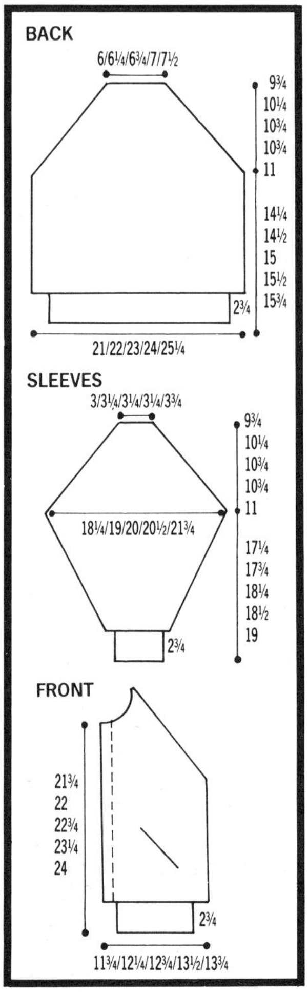

BACK
6/6¼/6¾/7/7½
9¾
10¼
10¾
10¾
11
14¼
14½
15
15½
15¾
2¾
21/22/23/24/25¼
SLEEVES
3/3¼/3¼/3¼/3¾
9¾
10¼
10¾
10¾
11
18¼/19/20/20½/21¾
17¼
17¾
18¼
18½
19
2¾
FRONT
21¾
22
22¾
23¼
24
2¾
11¾/12¼/12¾/13½/13¾

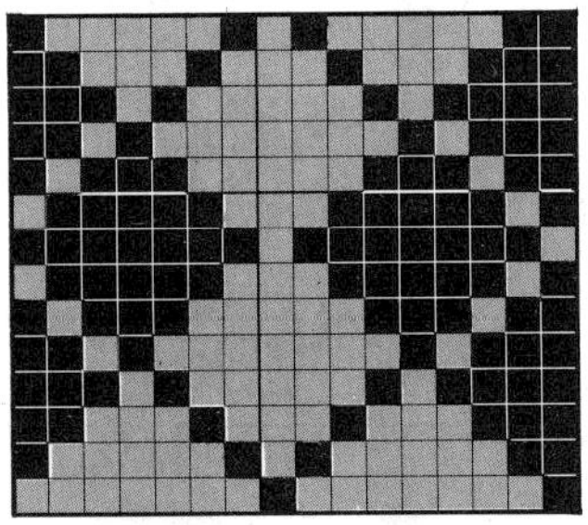

The small houndstooth chart should be incorporated into the sleeve.

Sleeves

Using No. 4 needles and ecru, cast on 51/53/55/57/59 sts. Work rib as for back, inc 8/10/10/12/12 sts evenly across last row of rib. Change to No. 6 needles and begin following houndstooth chart, repeating from beginning across the row and working in black and lilac. Keeping in pattern, inc 1 st at each end of the 3rd row and then every following 4th row 2/6/8/10/12 times. Then every following 5th row 18/15/14/13/12 times (101/107/111/117/121 sts). Cont to work even until sleeve measures 17¼/17¾/18¼/18½/19in from beg ending with a p row. **Shape raglan:** keeping in pattern, work as for back raglan shaping. Bind off remaining 17/19/19/21/21 sts.

Pocket linings

Using No. 6 needles and black, cast on 32/32/32/32/34 sts. Work in st st until work measures 4/4¼/4¼/4¼/4¾in ending with a p row. **Shape pocket slope:** dec 1 st at end of next row and at same edge on every following row until 2 sts remain. Work 1 row, bind off. Work second pocket in same manner, reversing shaping.

Pocket trims

Using No. 4 needles, black and with RS facing, pick up and knit 31/31/31/31/33 sts down lower edge of right pocket. Work in k1, p1 rib for 6 rows. Bind off in ribbing.

Right front

Using No. 4 needles and ecru, cast on 60/62/64/66/68 sts. Working in stripe sequence as for back, cont as follows:
Row 1: k5, sl 1, k5, p1, *k1, p1, rep from * to end.
Row 2: k1, *p1, k1, rep from * to last 11 sts, p to end.
Repeat these two rows until stripe sequence is complete, inc 6/7/8/9/10 sts evenly across last row of rib. Change to No. 6 needles and black and work in pattern as follows:
Row 1: k5, sl 1, k to end.
Row 2: purl.
Repeat these 2 rows 9 times more, then work chart 2, setting it up as follows: k5, sl 1, k10/12/14/16/18, k first row of chart, k to end. Work the chart in this position until it is complete. Work next row in p and cont in pattern until work measures 6¾/7/7/7/7½in from beg ending with a p row. **Shape pocket opening.** Row 1: k5, sl 1, k51/53/55/58/60 sts. Turn, leaving remaining sts on a holder.
Row 2: Purl.

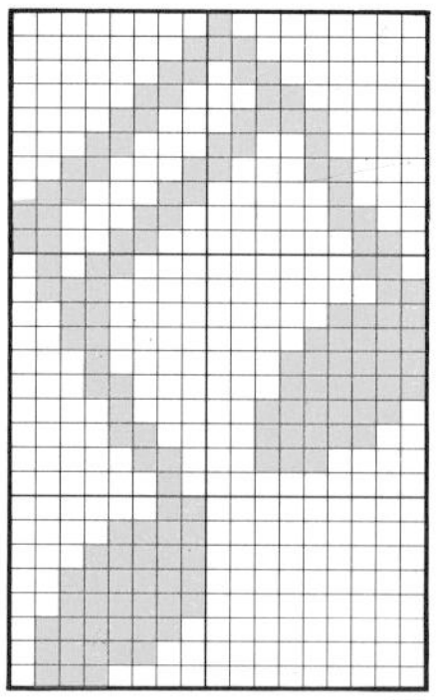
Chart 2

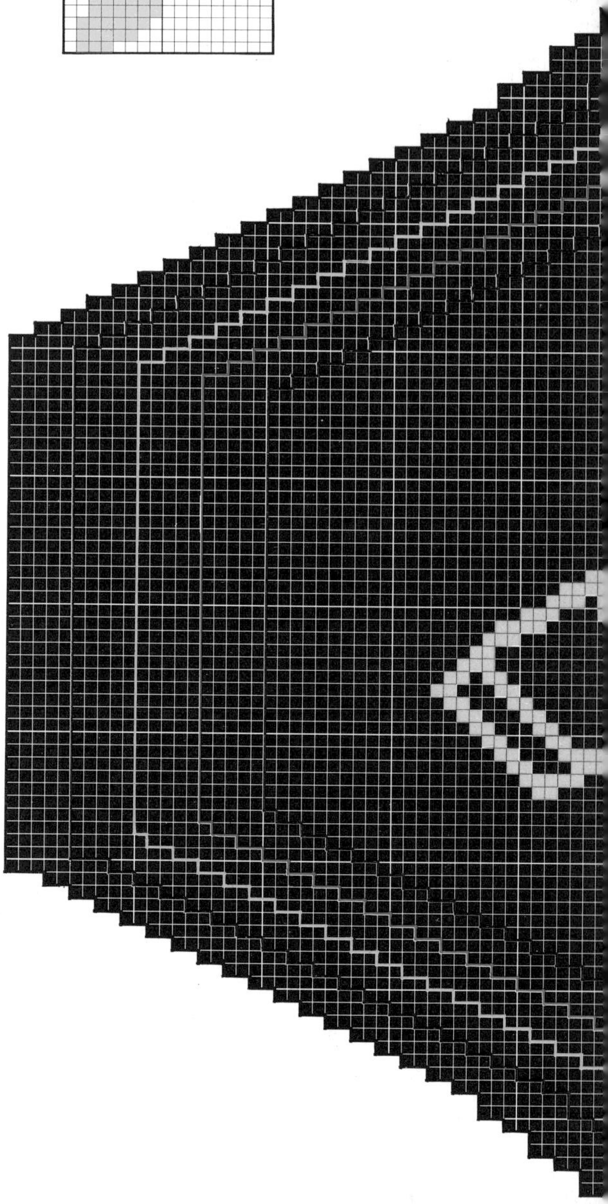

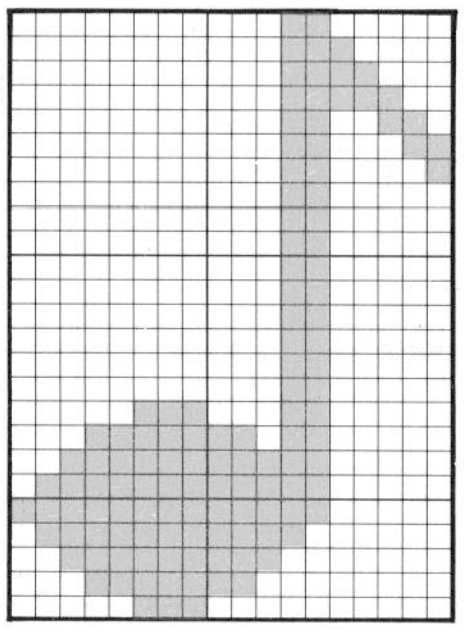
Chart 3

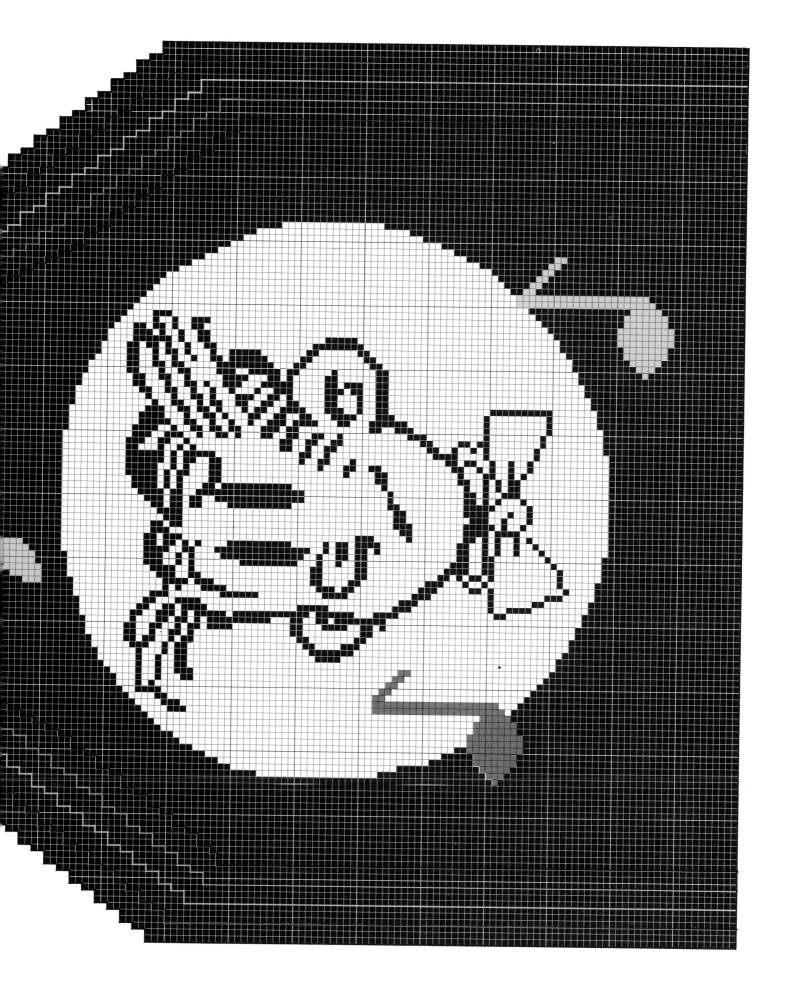

Row 3: k5, sl 1, k to last 4 sts, sktpo, k1.
Repeat 2nd and 3rd rows 15/15/15/15/16 times. Break yarn and leave remaining 25/27/29/32/32 sts on a holder. With RS facing, return to sts on first holder and, starting with a k row, cont in st st inc 1 st at beg of next row and at the same edge on every following row until there are 41/42/43/43/46 sts, ending with a p row. P across sts on second holder. Cont on all sts and in pattern until front measures 14¼/14½/15/15½/15¾in from beg, ending with a first row.
Shape raglan: bind off 2 sts at beg of next row.
Row 1: k5, sl 1, k to last 5 sts, ssk, k3.
Row 2: purl.
Row 3: k5, sl 1, k to last 6 sts, sktpo, k3.
Row 4: purl.
Repeat the last 4 rows 5/6/7/8/9 times, then repeat 2nd and 3rd rows 22/21/20/19/18 times. *At the same time* keep front edge even until front measures 21¾/22/22¾/23¼/24in, ending with a 2nd row. *And,* when raglan is decreased to 57/63/69/75/78 sts, begin chart 3 (*see* page 13), setting it up as follows: next row (RS): k10/12/14/16/18 sts, k first row of chart, k to end. Cont working chart in this position until it is complete.
When work measures 21¾/22/22¾/23¼/24in, **shape neck.** Next row (RS): bind off 14/15/16/17/18 sts at beg of next row and 2 sts at beg of next alt row. Work 1 row even. Dec 1 st at beg of next and every following row at the same edge 6 times. Keep neck edge even and cont with raglan shaping until 2 sts remain. Fasten off.

Left front
Work as for right front reversing shapings.
Work chart 3 (*see* page 12) only in pink.

Collar
Using No. 4 needles and black, cast on 151/161/169/175/183 sts. Work in k1, p1 rib for 1¼/1¼/1¼/2½/1½in. **Shape collar:** working in rib, bind off 4 sts at beg of next 8 rows. Bind off 5 sts at beg of next 14 rows and bind off 7/9/9/10/11 sts at beg of next 4 rows. Bind off remaining 21/23/29/33/37 sts.

Finishing
Join all raglan seams. Turn in front facings (*see* diagram) and stitch down. Stitch zipper in place. Sew shaped edge of collar to neck edge, sewing the straight edge of collar to the bound-off edge at beg of neck shaping. Turn collar to wrong side and slip stitch outside edge to inside edge. Join side and sleeve seams.

Fold back the right front along the dotted line, which indicates the line of sewn stitch, and sew A–B of the collar edge to A–B of the neck shaping. Sew the bound-off edge to the neck.

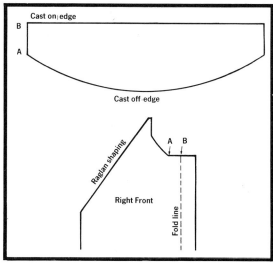

Betty Boop Sailor Jacket

Betty Boop and Pudgy are cruising off to fame and fortune in this light-weight worsted double-breasted jacket worked using the intarsia method (*see Techniques, page 7*). Instructions are given for four sizes to fit 6-, 8-, 10- and 12-year-olds.

Back

Using No. 4 needles and blue, cast on 70/76/82/88 sts.
Row 1: p1, *k1, p1, rep from * to end.
Row 2: k1, *p1, k1, rep from * to end.
Repeat these 2 rows until rib measures 2¾in, inc 8 sts evenly across last row of rib 78/84/90/96 sts. Change to No. 6 needles and white and, starting with a k row, work in st st (3 rows white, 5 rows blue) twice, then 3 rows white. Change to blue, work 2/2/20/20 rows. Then begin reading chart and setting it up as follows: k6/9/12/15 sts, k first row of chart, k6/9/12/15 sts. Cont working chart in this position until it is complete. *At the same time,* when work measures 9/10¼/11/12¼in, **shape armholes.** Bind off 3/4/5/6 sts at beg of next 2 rows. Cont to work even until work measures 16¼, 17¾, 19, 20½in from beg, ending with a p row. **Shape shoulders:** bind off 7/7/8/8 sts at beg of next 2 rows, 7/7/8/8 sts

Materials
Melinda Coss light-weight worsted cotton – royal blue (main color): 16/18/18/20oz; white: 3½oz; all other colors to match chart: less than 1¾oz of each.
6 silver buttons, approx ¾in in diameter.

Needles
One pair of No. 4 and one pair of No. 6 needles; one 16in circular needle.

Gauge
Using No. 6 needles and measured over st st, 22 sts and 28 rows = 4in square.

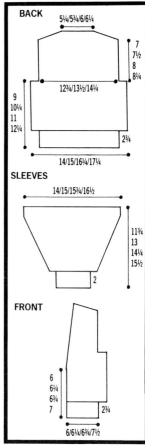

Work the chart into the back of the jacket, positioning it as described on page 15.

at beg of the following 2 rows, and 7/8/8/8 sts at beg of next 2 rows. Bind off remaining 30/32/34/36 sts.

Left front
Using No. 4 needles and blue, cast on 29/33/35/39 sts. Work in k1, p1 rib as for back for 2¾in, inc 4/3/4/3 sts evenly across last row of rib 33/36/39/42 sts. Change to No. 6 needles and white and work stripe sequence as for back. Then cont in main color only, until work measures 6/6¼/6¾/7in from beg, ending with a k row. **Shape front slope:** dec

1 st at beg of next row and every following 7th row at the same edge 8/9/10/11 times. *At the same time*, work side edge even until work measures 9/10¼/11/12¼in from the beg, ending with a p row. **Shape armholes:** bind off 3/4/5/6 sts at beg of next row. When all the shaping has been completed and 21/22/23/24 sts remain, cont to work even until work measures 16¼/17¾/19/20in, ending with a p row. **Shape shoulder:** bind off 7/7/7/8 sts at beg of next row and 7/7/8/8 sts at beg of the following alt row. Work 1 row even. Bind off remaining 7/8/8/8 sts.

Right front
Work to match left front, reversing shapings.

Left sleeve
Using No. 4 needles and blue, cast on 37/41/43/47 sts. Work in rib as for back for 2in, inc 9/9/11/11 sts evenly across last row of rib (46/50/54/58 sts). Change to No. 6 needles and, starting with a k row, begin working stripe sequence as for back in st st, inc 1 st at each end of every 3rd row 4/0/0/0 times, then every 4th row 12/17/9/0 times, then every 5th row 0/0/8/17 times (78/84/88/92 sts). *At the same time*, when 7 rows of blue have been

This chart should be worked into the left sleeve.

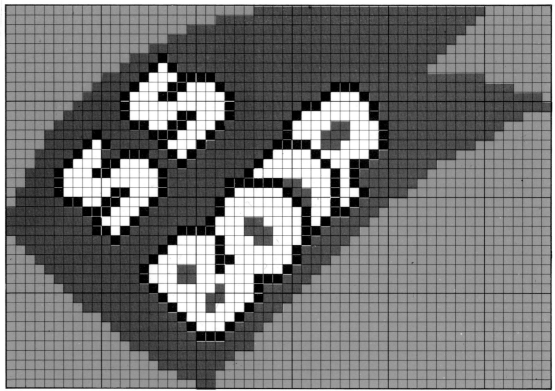

completed following the last white stripe, set up chart as follows. Next row (RS): k1/2/4/5 sts, k first row of flag chart. K2/3/5/6 sts. Cont working chart in this position until it is complete. When increases are completed, you should have 78/84/88/92 sts on your needle. Cont to work even until work measures 11¾/13/14¼/15½in from beg. Bind off loosely.

Right sleeve
Work as for left sleeve omitting chart.

Finishing and collar
Join shoulder seams. With RS facing and using a 16in circular needle and blue, start at the lower edge and pick up and k 36/39/42/45 sts up right front to start of front slope, 73/81/87/95 sts up right front slope to shoulder, 30/32/34/36 sts across back neck, 72/80/86/94 sts down left front slope, and 36/39/42/45 sts down left front to lower edge (247/271/291/315 sts). Working backwards and forwards in rows on the circular needle, work in rib as for back starting with a 2nd row. Work 1 row keeping rib pattern as established and shape collar as follows: Row 1 (RS): rib 109/121/131/143 sts, *k1, p1, k1 into next st, rib 3, rep from * 6 times, k1, p1, k1 into next st, rib 1, turn.

Row 2: sl 1, rib 46/50/54/58, turn.
Row 3: sl 1, rib 58/62/66/70, turn.
Row 4: sl 1, rib 70/74/78/82, turn.
Continue in this manner working 12 sts more than on previous row until you have worked a row of sl 1, rib 166/170/174/178.
Next row: sl 1, rib to end.
Next row: rib across all sts, ending with a WS row (263/287/307/341 sts). Work 2 rows in rib.
Next row (buttonhole row: rib 4, * bind off 3, rib 11/12/13/14, rep from * once, bind off 3, rib to end.
Next row: rib to end, casting on 3 sts over those bound off on previous row. Work 12 rows. Repeat the 2 buttonhole rows once more, then work 2 rows even. **Shape front edge.** Next row: rib 223/233/243/253, turn.
Next row: sl 1, rib 182/192/202/212, turn.
Next row: sl 1, rib 174/184/194/204, turn.
Cont in this way, working 8 sts less than on previous row until you have worked a row of sl 1, rib 126/136/146/156.
Next row: sl 1, rib to end.
Next row: rib across all sts. Bind off in ribbing.

Finishing
Join sleeves to jacket. Join side and sleeve seams. Sew on buttons.

Wimpy Aran Sweater

Wimpy is a master con-artist, a professional layabout who has never worked a day in his life. With an IQ of 326, his only interest in life is persuading his friends to buy him enough hamburgers to satisfy his insatiable appetite. This snug, heavy-weight worsted sweater is suitable for boys and girls and the pattern is quoted in four sizes.

Materials
Melinda Coss heavy-weight worsted – ecru: 20oz; black: 3½oz; gold: 3½oz; red, blue, tan, brown and flesh: 1¾oz of each.

Needles
One pair of No. 7 and one pair of No. 9 needles.

Gauge
Using No. 9 needles and worked over st st, 17 sts and 21 rows = 4in square.

The chart (left) should be used to complete the sleeves (*see* page 23), and the chart overleaf (page 20) should be worked to complete the front. The colored lines indicate the areas to be worked for the various sizes.

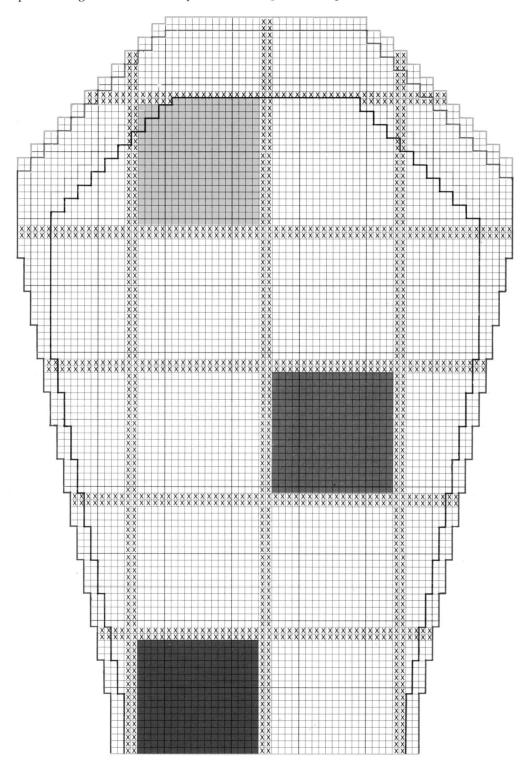

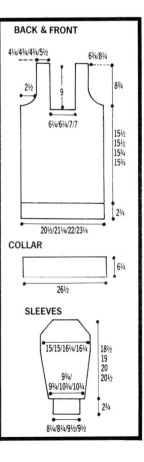

19

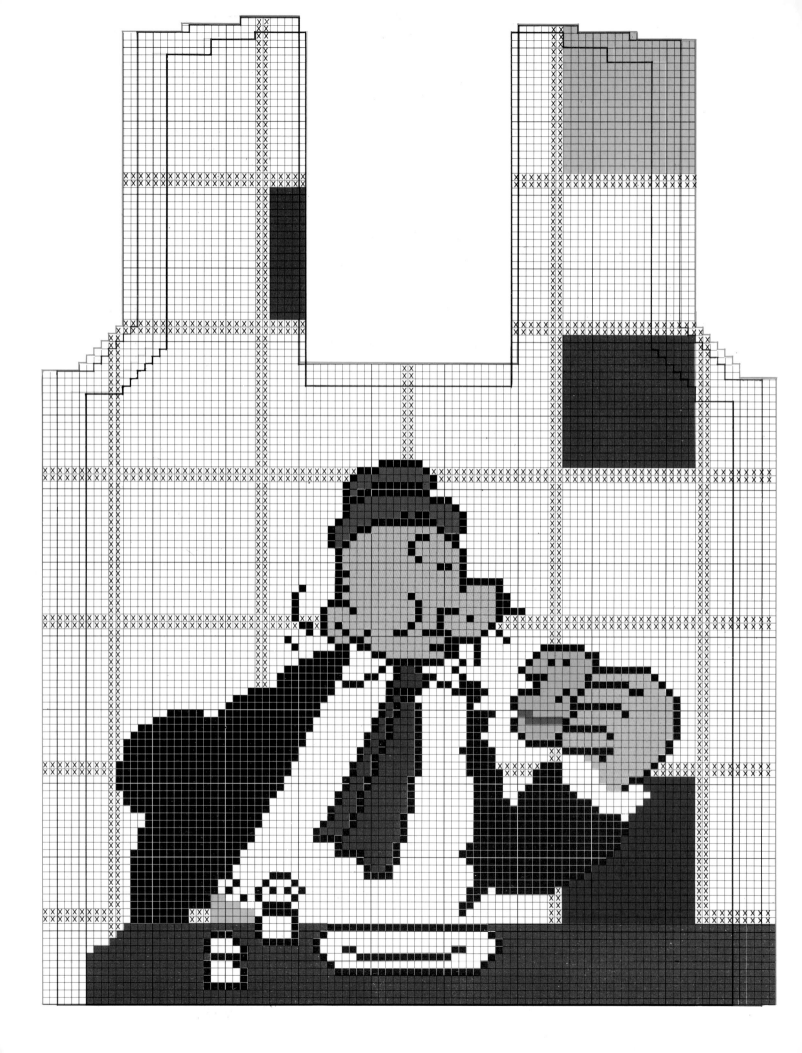

Back

Using No. 7 needles and ecru, cast on 88/92/96/100 sts. Work 15 rows in k1, p1 rib. Change to No. 9 needles and begin following chart in st st with the exception of the X symbol which should be worked in main color in reverse st st – i.e., k on a purl row and p on a knit row. Work to armhole shaping. Cont to follow chart, bind off 5 sts at beg of next 2 rows, * dec 1 st at each end of the next 6 rows (66/70/74/78 sts). Cont following chart to shoulder shaping. Bind off 6/7/7/8 sts at beg of next 4 rows, then bind off 7/7/7/8 sts at beg of next 2 rows. Bind off remaining 28/28/30/30 sts.

Front

Work as for back to *. **Shape neck:** dec 1 st, work 24/26/27/29 sts. Bind off 28/28/30/30 sts, work to last 2 sts, dec 1 st. Work on last set of sts only, dec 1 st at armhole edge on next 5 rows. Cont following chart to shoulder shaping.
Shape shoulders: bind off 6/7/7/8 sts at beg of next and following alt row. Work 1 row even. Bind off remaining sts. Rejoin yarn to inner edge of remaining sts and work to match other side.

Sleeves

Using No. 7 needles and ecru, cast on 36/36/40/40 sts and work 14 rows in k1, p1 rib, inc 6 sts evenly across last row (42/42/46/46 sts). Change to No. 9 needles and begin following chart, inc 1 st at each end of the 9th row and every following 5th row, until you have 64/64/74/74 sts. Cont following chart to sleeve cap shaping: bind off 2 sts at beg of every row until 28/28/30/30 sts remain. Bind off loosely.

Collar

Using ecru and No. 7 needles, cast on 114/114/122/122 sts. Work 6in in k1, p1 rib. Change to black and rib for 2 rows. Bind off.

Finishing

Using a flat seam throughout, join shoulder, side and sleeve seams. Carefully set in sleeves. Sew cast-on edge of collar around neck. Sew short edges to front opening, crossing the collar left over right.

The chart opposite (page 22) should be worked to complete the back of the sweater. Follow the appropriate color for the size you are making.

Pudgy Baby's Blouson

Materials
Melinda Coss light-weight worsted wool – red: 7/9/9oz; black: 1¾oz; other colors to match chart: 1¾oz of each. A separating zipper measuring 9½/10½/12in. If you have trouble finding the right size separating zipper, special zippers can be ordered from Feibusch Zippers, 33 Allen Street, New York, NY 10002; telephone: (212) 226-3964. This store carries nylon separating zippers in all types and styles and in a wide variety of colors for about $5 each. Inquire about price and shipping.

Needles
One pair of No. 2 and one pair of No. 5 needles.

Gauge
Using No. 5 needles and measured over st st, 23 sts and 30 rows = 4in square. Ribs worked on No. 2 needles.

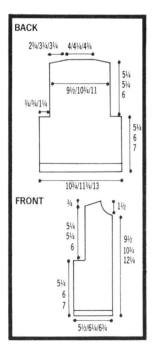

Work the chart opposite (page 25) into the back of the jacket.

Betty Boop's pal, Pudgy, sports his favorite jacket ready to go to the baseball match. The jacket is worked in light-weight worsted yarn using the intarsia method (*see* Techniques, page 7).

Back
Using No. 2 needles and black, cast on 63/69/75 sts and work 2 rows of k1, p1 rib. Change to red, work 6 rows, change back to black and work 2 rows. Change to No. 5 needles and red and begin following chart to armhole shaping. Bind off 4/4/6 sts at beg of next 2 rows. Work even to shoulder shapings. Bind off 5/6/6 sts at beg of next 4 rows and 6 sts at beg of next 2 rows. Bind off remaining 23/25/27 sts.

Right front
Using No. 2 needles and black, cast on 33/37/39 sts and work rib as for back. Change to No. 5 needles and red and work in st st until front matches back to armhole shaping. Bind off 4/4/6 sts at beg of next row, then cont on the remaining 29/33/33 sts until work measures 9½/10¾/12¼ in from beg, ending at front edge.

Shape neck: bind off 4/5/5 sts at beg of next row, 2 sts at neck edge on the next 2/3/3 alt rows and 1 st on next 5/4/4 alt rows. When front matches back to shoulder shaping, bind off 5/6/6 sts at beg of next row and the following alt row. Work 1 row even and bind off remaining 6 sts.

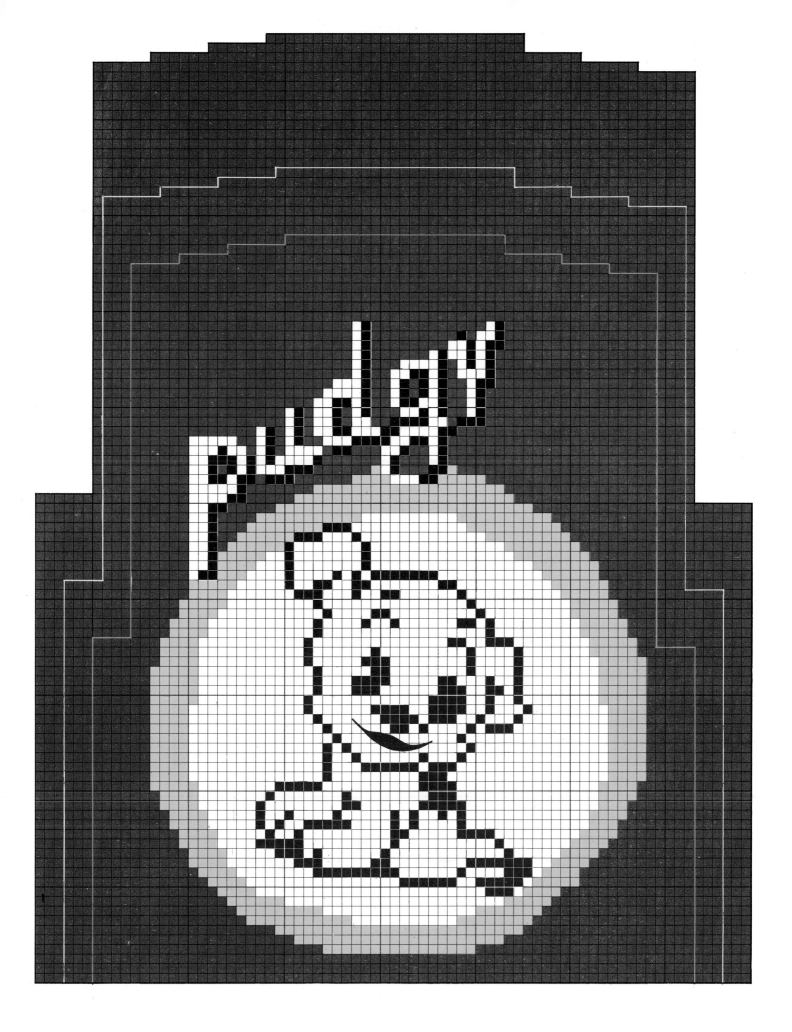

a WS row. Change to black. Work 3 rows in k1, p1 rib. Bind off in ribbing.

Collar

Using No. 2 needles and red, cast on 27/31/33 sts. Work 1 row of k1, p1 rib. Working rib pattern as established, cast on 4 sts at beg of every row 10 times. *At the same time*, when 6 rows red have been worked, change to black and work 2 rows. Work 2 rows red and 1 row black. Work one more row black without shaping, then 1 row red. Cont in red only, bind off 4 sts at beg of next 10 rows. Work 1 row even, then bind off remaining 27/31/33 sts.

Finishing

Join shoulder seams. Join sleeves to armholes using a narrow backstitch. Join side and sleeve seams. Slip stitch pockets to fronts, placing them 1in in from side seams and directly above rib. Sew cast-on edge of collar neatly around neck edge, fold in half (WS together) and slip st bound-off edge into place. Embroider the mouth using backstitch. Sew zipper firmly to front edges.

HAT

Using No. 2 needles, cast on 77/90/99 sts in red. Work in 4 row stripes of k1, p1 rib, alternating between red and black. Cont until work measures 6¾in. Complete stripe and cut yarn leaving a long end. Thread yarn back through sts and gather. Secure firmly. Sew side seam, taking care to match stripes. Make a pompon (*see* Techniques, page 9) and stitch firmly to top of hat.

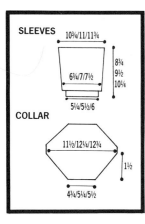

SLEEVES

10¾/11/11¾

8¾
9½
10¼

6¾/7/7½

5¼/5½/6

COLLAR

11½/12¼/12¾

1½

4¾/5¼/5½

Left front

Work as for right front, reversing shapings.

Sleeves

Using No. 2 needles and black, cast on 31/33/35 sts and work in rib as for back, inc 8/8/8 sts evenly across last row of rib (39/41/43 sts). Change to No. 5 needles and cont in st st, inc 1 st at each end of every 6th row 10/11/11 times, then the following 4th row 1/1/2 times. Work even until sleeve measures 8/8¾/9½ in, change to black and work in st st for 3 rows. Bind off in black.

Pockets (Make 2)

Using No. 5 needles and red, cast on 23 sts and work in st st for 2/2½/2½in ending with

I Y'am What I Y'am

A man-size Popeye sweater for spinach lovers worked using the intarsia method (*see* Techniques, page 7). Knitted in a heavy-weight worsted yarn, this drop-sleeved crew-necked, stripy number should enhance the muscles of any strong seafaring man.

Back

Using No. 7 needles and blue, cast on 100 sts. Work in k2, p2 rib for 2¾in. Change to No. 9 needles and white and cont in st st, working in stripes of 10 rows white, 10 rows blue, until you have completed 13 stripes. Now work 6 rows blue and cont in stripe sequence, working as follows. **Shape neck:** next row: k 42 sts, leave remaining sts on a spare needle and work on this first set of sts only. Turn, bind off 5 sts, p to end. Dec 1 st at neck edge on next 6 rows, work one row even, leave remaining 31 sts on a holder. Rejoin yarn to remaining sts and bind off center 16 sts. K to end, turn, p back. Bind off 5 sts at beginning of next row, then bind off 1 st at neck edge on next 6 rows. Leave remaining 31 sts on a holder.

Front

Work as for back in the same stripe sequence but following the chart for front. Shape neck as for back, leaving shoulder sts on holders.

Sleeves

Using No. 7 needles and blue, cast on 40 sts and work in k2, p2 rib for 2¾in. Change to No. 9 needles and white and cont in st st working in 10 row stripe sequence as for body but inc 1 st at each end of every 4th row until you have 80 sts. *At the same time,* when 16 rows of st st have been worked, begin anchor motif as follows: keeping in stripe squence as established, k17, knit first row of chart, k17. Cont working chart in this position until it is complete, then cont in stripe sequence only until you have 80 sts. You are now on a blue stripe. Work even until this stripe and one more white stripe are complete. Bind off loosely.

Neckband

With RS of back and front facing each other, knit shoulder seams together. Using a 16in circular needle and blue, pick up and knit 84 sts evenly around the neck. Work in rounds of k2, p2 rib in blue until neckband measures 3in. Bind off loosely, fold neckband in half to wrong side and slip st bound-off edge to pick-up edge.

Finishing

Join sleeves to body using a very narrow backstitch. Join sleeve and body seams with a flat seam taking care to match stripes. If wished, embroider "Spinach" on the tin.

Materials

Melinda Coss heavy-weight worsted – royal blue: 13oz; white: 11oz; black: 1¾oz; flesh, yellow, emerald, tan and grey: less than 1¾oz of each.

Needles

One pair of No. 7 and one pair of No. 9 needles; one 16in circular needle.

Gauge

Using No. 9 needles and measured over st st, 17 sts and 21 rows = 4in square. Ribs worked on No. 7 needles.

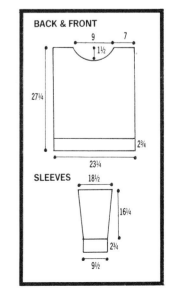

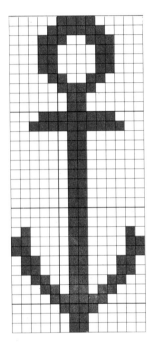

Incorporate the anchor chart
(above) into both sleeves and
the chart opposite (page 29)
into the front.

Olive Oyl's Dress

Materials
Melinda Coss light-weight
worsted wool – blue (main
color): 13oz; emerald,
white and black: 3½oz of
each; all other colors to
match chart: less than
1¾oz of each.

Needles
One pair of No. 4 and
one pair of No. 6 needles.

Gauge
Using No. 6 needles and
measured over st st, 22
sts and 30 rows = 4in
square. Ribs worked on
No. 4 needles.

In her usual delicate manner, Olive Oyl calls
for Popeye. A skinny dress for howlers
worked in stockinette stitch, using light-
weight worsted wool and the intarsia
method (*see* Techniques, page 7).

Back
Using No. 4 needles and blue, cast on
103 sts.
Row 1: *k1, p1, rep from * to end, k1.
Row 2: *p1, k1, rep from * to end, p1. Rep
these 2 rows once more.
Change to No. 6 needles and, starting with
a k row, begin reading chart and working in
st st to armhole shaping. **Shape armholes:**
bind off 5 sts at beg of next 2 rows. Bind off
1 st at beg of next 12 rows. ** Cont to work
even to shoulder shapings. Bind off 6 sts at
beg of next 6 rows. Bind off 5 sts at beg of
next 2 rows. Bind off remaining 35 sts.

Front
Work as for back to **. Cont to work even to
neck shaping. Next row (RS): k34, slip
remaining sts onto a spare needle and work
on this first set of sts only. Bind off 3 sts at
neck edge on next row, 2 sts on next 3 alt
rows, 1 st on next alt row. **Shape shoulder**:
bind off 6 sts at beg of next row, dec 1 st at
neck edge on next row, bind off 6 sts at
shoulder edge on following row. Working
even at neck edge, bind off 6 sts at shoulder

edge on next alt row, work 1 row even, bind
off remaining 5 sts. Rejoin yarn to front
neck, bind off center 13 sts, work to end,
work 1 row even. Shape to match other side.

Sleeves
Using No. 4 needles and blue, cast on 64 sts.
Work in k1, p1 rib for 4 rows, inc 15 sts
evenly across last row of rib (79 sts). Change
to No. 6 needles and work even in blue only
until sleeve measures 6¾in, ending with a
WS row. **Shape cap:** bind off 5 sts at beg of
next 2 rows, dec 1 st at each end of the next
and every alt row until 46 sts remain, ending
with a WS row. Bind off 2 sts at beg of next
8 rows, 3 sts at beg of next 4 rows, then 4 sts
at beg of next 2 rows. Bind off remaining 10
sts.

Neckband
Join one shoulder seam. Using No. 4 needles
and blue, pick up and knit 86 sts evenly
around neck. Work in k1, p1 rib for 4 rows.
Bind off in ribbing.

Finishing
Press lightly. Join second shoulder seam and
seam neckband edges with a flat seam. Stitch
sleeve caps in place, join side and sleeve
seams using flat seams throughout.

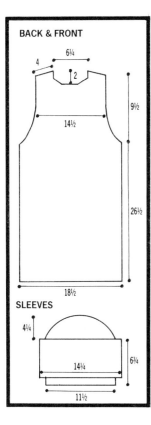

The charts on pages 32 and 33 should be used to complete the front of the dress, those on pages 34 and 35, the back of the dress.

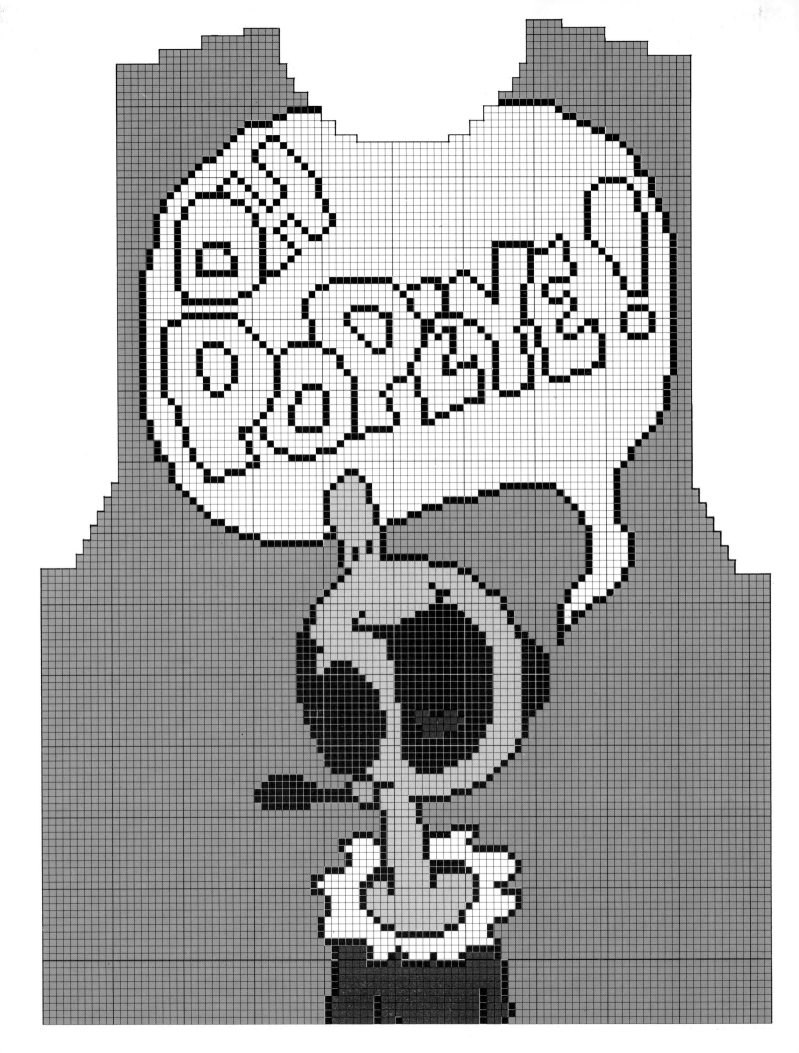

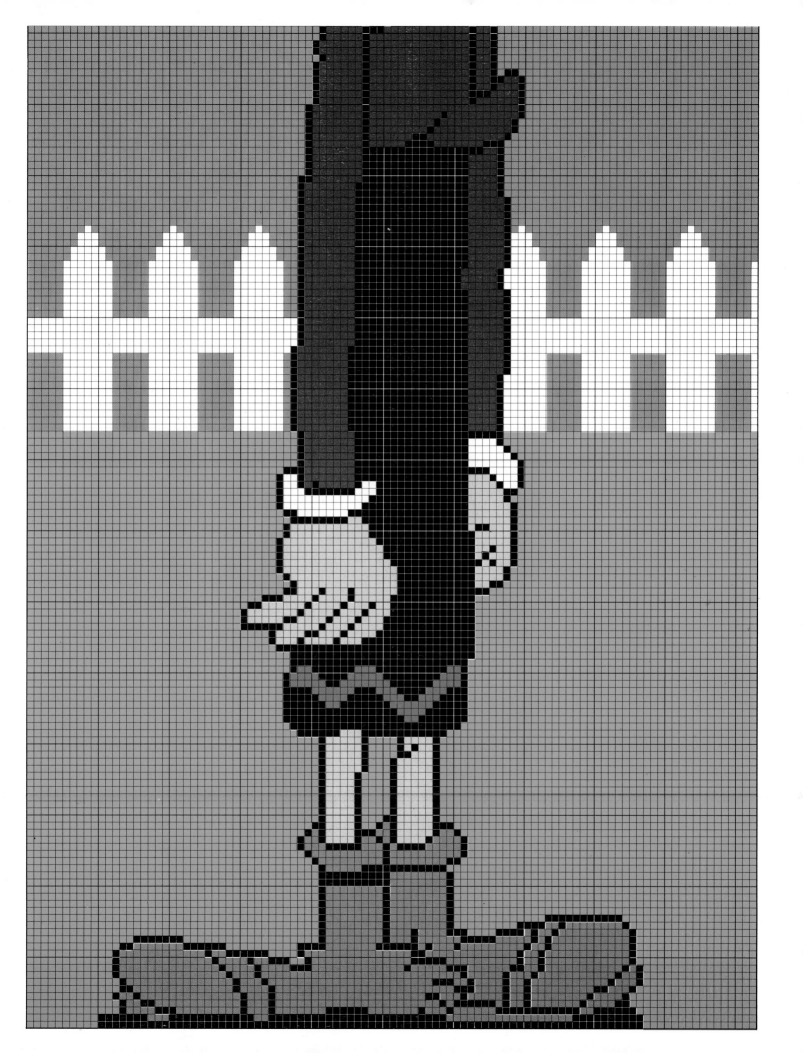

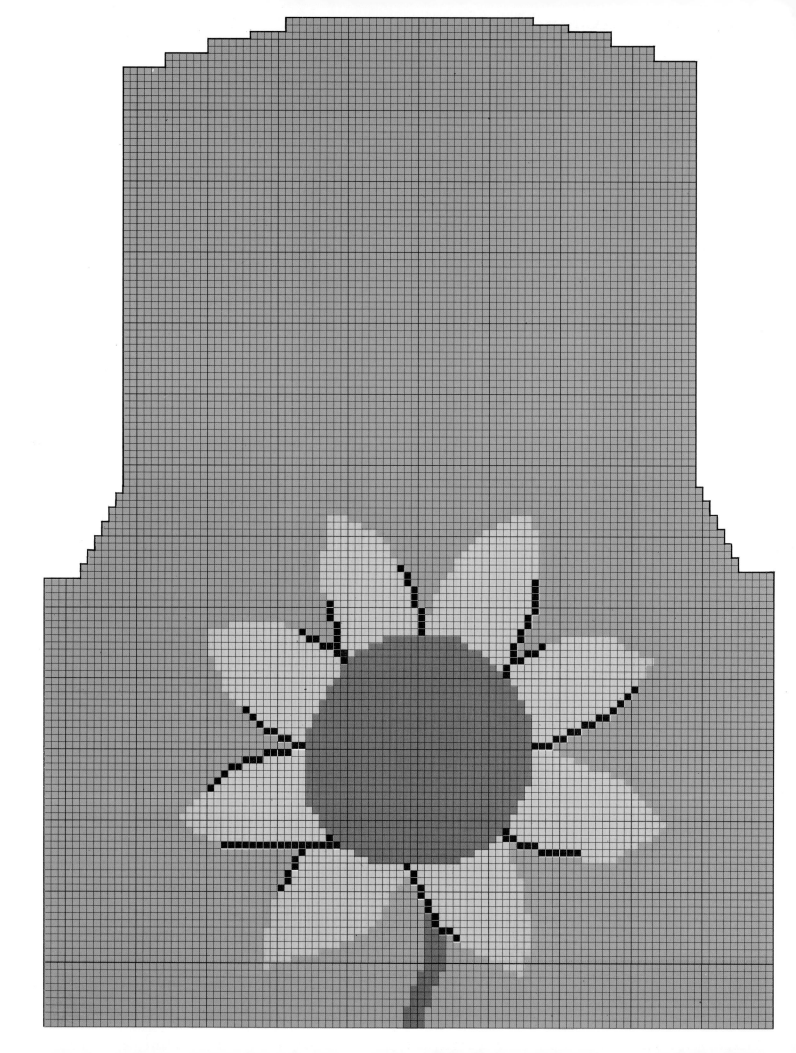

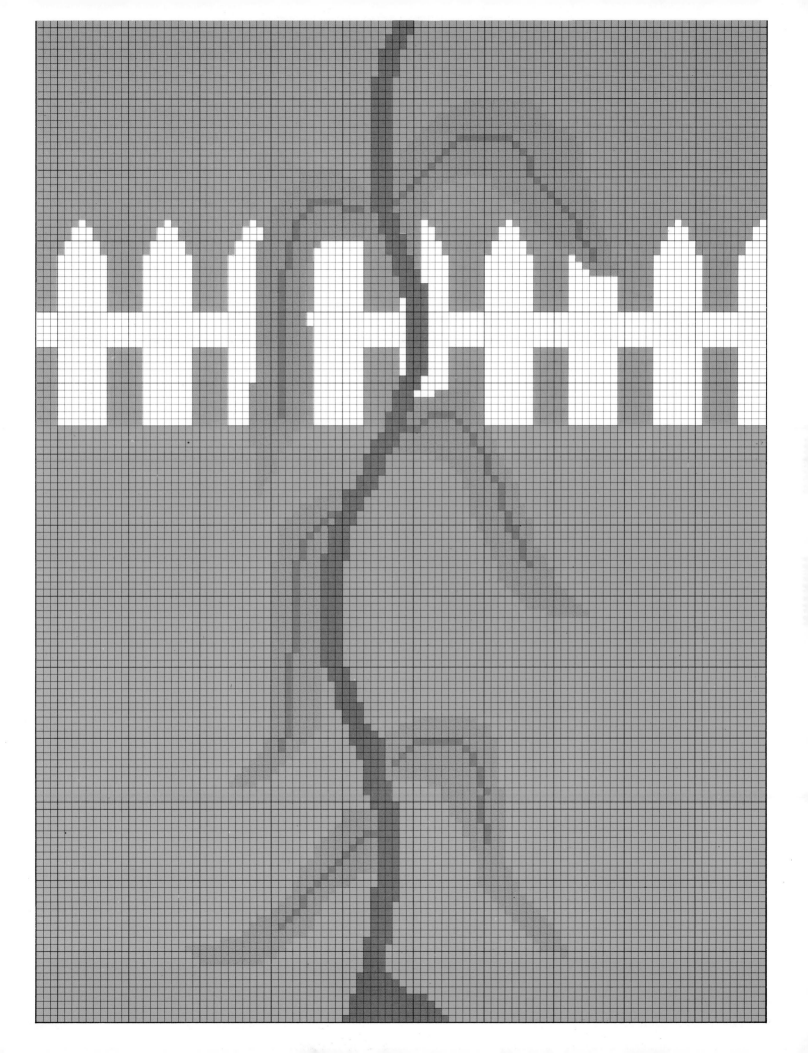

Popeye's son is a little rascal with a nose for trouble. Popeye keeps him healthy on a diet of spinach and his greatest ambition in life is to need a haircut.

Shown in two sizes to fit children aged 9 months and 1 year, this three piece is worked in garter and stockinette stitch in fingering-weight wool.

BIB OVERALLS

Back

Left leg Using No. 2 needles and white, cast on 27/29 sts. Work in k1, p1 rib for ¼in, inc once into every st on last row of rib (54/57 sts).

Change to No. 3 needles and work in garter st. Knit every row, working in alternate stripes of 2 rows white and 2 rows blue until work measures 9/9¾in, ending with a WS row. * Dec 2 sts at beg of next row. Work 1 row and leave this piece of work on a holder.

Right leg Work as for left leg to * but end with a first row. Next row: bind off 2 sts, knit to end. Next row: k52/55 sts, then, beg at shaped edge, k52/55 sts from left leg. Work one more stripe on these 104/110 sts.

Shape body: k49/52, k2 tog, k2, sl 1, k1, psso, k49/52. Cont to dec in this way on each side of the center 2 sts on the next 6 alt rows (90/96 sts), then work even until work measures 17/18¼in, ending with a RS row of a blue stripe. Dec 15 sts evenly across next row (75/81 sts). Still using No. 3 needles, work 8 rows in k1, p1 rib in white and cont in st st and white only.

Bib

Row 1: k19/22 sts. K RS row of chart, k to end.

Row 2: p19/22 sts, p WS row of chart, p to end. Cont in st st, working chart in this position for another 6 rows. Cont to follow chart and shape armholes as follows: bind off 4/5 sts at beg of next 2 rows, 3 sts at beg of next 2 rows, 2 sts at beg of next 4 rows and l st at beg of next 6 rows. Then dec 1 st at each end of the following 4th row and the following 8th row. Work 4 more rows in st st, then work 6 rows in k1, p1 rib. Bind off in ribbing.

Front

Work as for back.

Armband shoulder straps (Make 2)

Using No. 2 needles and white, cast on 6 sts working in garter st and in two-row stripe sequence as for legs. Cont until work measures 12¾/15in. Make buttonhole. K2, k2 tog, k2. Next row: k2, inc 1, k2. Work 4 more rows. Bind off.

Finishing

Using black wool, embroider features on Swee' pea's face as shown on the chart. Join side seams, taking care to match stripes. Stitch armbands neatly around armhole with buttonholes at the back (back strap overlaps front strap by ¾in). Sew on button

Materials

Melinda Coss fingering weight wool – white: 10oz; blue: 6oz; less than 1oz of each of red, flesh and black to match chart. 1½ft fine-weight elastic. 7 buttons approximately ½in in diameter.

Needles

One pair of No.2 and one pair of No.3 needles.

Gauge

Using No. 3 needles and measured over st st, 30 sts and 40 rows = 4in square. Ribs worked on No. 2 needles.

Work the chart opposite (page 39) into the bib as described on page 37.

positioning to fit, approximately ¾in down from top of straps.

HAT

Using No. 3 needles and white, cast on 230 sts. Work in two row stripes of white and blue garter st throughout. Work 18 rows. Next row: k2 tog to end (115 sts). Work 2 rows.

Next row: k twice into every alt st (172 sts). Work 34 more rows, ending on a second row. **Shape crown:** dec 1 st at each end of next row.

Next row: *k15, k2 tog, rep from * to end (160 sts). K next row.

Next row: *k14, k2 tog, rep from * to end. K next row. Cont to dec in this way until 10 sts remain. Break yarn leaving a long end and thread through the remaining sts. Sew up side seam. Securely fasten top thread. Weave elastic through center decrease row.

CARDIGAN

Body (Worked in one piece)
Using No. 2 needles and white, cast on 155/167 sts.

Work in k1, p1 rib for 1¼in, inc 1 st at the center of the last row of rib (156/168 sts). Change to No. 3 needles and work in two-row stripes of garter st until work measures 6¼/7in, ending with a WS row. **Divide for armholes:** next row: k39/42, turn and cont on these sts for right front leaving remaining sts on a holder. **Shape raglan:** dec 1 st at beg of next row and the next 23/25 alt rows (keep front edge even) until work measures 9½/10in, ending at front edge. **Shape neck:** bind off 6/7 sts at beg of next row, 3 sts at same edge on next alt row, 2 sts on following alt row and 1 st on next 2 alt rows. Cont to dec raglan until 2 sts remain. Bind off.

With RS facing, rejoin yarn to held sts and k78/84 sts, turn, and cont on these sts for back. Dec 1 st at each end of next row and next 25/27 alt rows. Bind off remaining 26/28 sts for back neck.

Left front
Return to remaining 39/42 sts. With RS facing, rejoin yarn and k to end. Complete as for right front reversing shapings.

Right sleeve
Using No. 2 needles and white, cast on 44/50 sts and work in k1, p1 rib for 1¼ in. Inc

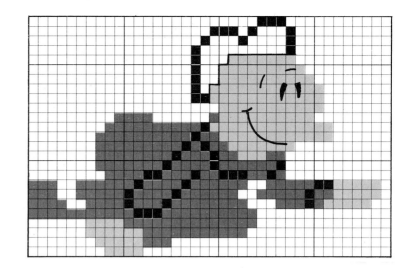

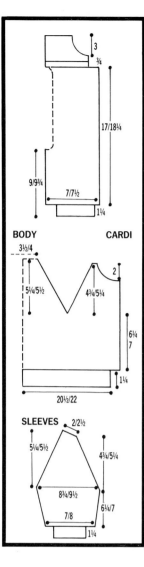

BODY   **CARDI**

SLEEVES

10 sts evenly along last row of rib (54/60 sts). Change to No. 3 needles and work in st st two-row stripes of garter st, inc 1 st at each end of every 7th row, 6 times. Work even on 66/72 sts until work measures 6¼/7in, ending with a WS row. **Raglan shaping:** dec 1 st at beg of next 48/52 rows. Bind off 5/6 sts at beg of next row (front edge), then dec 1 st at beg of following row (back edge). Repeat last 2 rows once more. Bind off remaining 6 sts.

Left sleeve
Work as for right sleeve reversing shapings.

Front border
Using No. 2 needles and white, cast on 9 sts.
Row 1: k1, p1 to last st, k1.
Row 2: p1, k1 to last st, p1.
Cont in rib until buttonband fits front edge when slightly stretched.

Buttonhole band
Cast on 9 sts and work in rib as for front border. When 8/4 rows have been worked, work buttonhole as follows: rib 4, bind off 2, rib to end. Next row: cast on 2 sts over those bound off. Space 4 more buttonholes evenly along the band. When band matches front border in length, bind off.

Finishing
Match raglan sleeves to body raglan shaping and join, using a flat seam and leaving bound-off edges of top of sleeves to form part of neckline. Sew front borders into place with buttonhole band on the right for girls and left for boys.

Neck ruffle
Using No. 3 needles and white, cast on 13 sts.
Row 1: k.
Row 2: p9, turn, k9, turn, p9, turn, k9, turn, p9, k4.
Row 3: k.
Row 4: p9, k4.
Rep these 4 rows until the straight garter stitch edges fit right around the neck, beginning and ending at the inside edge of the buttonbands. Lightly press the ruffled edge and stitch to neck.

Popeye's Guernsey

A seafaring sweater for more ambitious knitters. Worked in a combination of aran pattern work and fairisle, this sweater is knitted in worsted weight wool with instructions given in three sizes.

STITCH PATTERNS

The anchor (Worked in a panel of 32 sts)
Row 1: purl.
Row 2: knit.

Row 3: p15, k2, p15.
Row 4: k15, p2, k15.
Row 5: p14, sl next st to cn and hold at back. K1, then k1 from cn, sl next st to cn and hold at front. K1, then k1 from cn, p14.
Row 6: k13, fc, p2, bc, k13.
Row 7: p12, bc, p1, k2, p1, fc, p12.
Row 8: k11, fc, k2, p2, k2, bc, k11.
Row 9: p10, bc, p3, k2, p3, fc, p10.
Row 10: k9, fc, k4, p2, k4, bc, k9.
Row 11: p8, bc, p5, k2, p5, fc, p8.

Materials
Melinda Coss worsted weight wool – ecru: 27oz; coral 1¾oz; all other colors to match the chart: less than 1¾oz of each.

Needles
One pair of No. 4 and one pair of No. 5 needles.

Gauge
Using No. 5 needles and measured over st st, 26 sts and 30 rows = 4in square. Ribs worked on No. 4 needles.

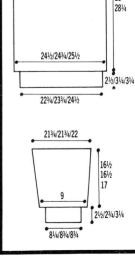

Incorporate the chart opposite (page 43) into the back and front of the guernsey.

Row 12: k7, fc, k6, p2, k6, bc, k7.
Row 13: p6, bc, p7, k2, p7, fc, p6.
Row 14: k5, fc, k8, p2, k8, bc, k5.
Row 15: p4, bc, p9, k2, p9, fc, p4.
Row 16: k1, p1, (k2, p1) twice, k7, p2, k7, (p1, k2) twice, p1, k.
Row 17: p1, fc, p1, k1, p1, bc, p7, k2, p7, fc, p1, k1, p1, bc, p1.
Row 18: k2, (p1, k1 twice), p1, k8, (p1, k1 twice), p1, k2.
Row 19: p2, fc, k1, bc, p8, k2, p8, fc, k1, bc, p2.
Row 20: k3, p3, k9, p2, k9, p2, k3.
Row 21: p3, m1, sl 1, k2 tog, psso, k1, p9, k2, p9, m1, sl 1, k2 tog, psso, m1, p3.
Row 22: k4, p1, k10, p2, k10, p1, k4.
Row 23: p10, MB, p4, k2, p4, MB, p10.
Row 24: k10, p1b, k4, p2, k4, p1b, k10.
Row 25: p10, fc, p3, k2, p3, bc, p10.
Row 26: k11, bc, k2, p2, k2, fc, k11.
Row 27: p12, fc, p1, k2, p1, bc, p12.
Row 28: k13, bc, p2, fc, k13.
Row 29: p14, fc, pc, p14.
Row 30: rep row 4.
Row 31: p15, sl next st to cn and hold in front, k1, then k1 from cn, p15.
Row 32: k14, fc, bc, k14.
Row 33: p13, bc, p2, fc, p13.
Row 34: k12, fc, k4, bc, k12.

Row 35: p12, k1, p6, k1, p12.
Row 36: k12, p1, k6, p1, k12.
Row 37: p12, fc, p4, bc, p12.
Row 38: k13, bc, k2, fc, k13.
Row 39: p14, fc, bc, p14.
Row 40: k15, skip 1 st and purl the 2nd st, then purl the skipped st and slip both sts from needle tog, k15.
Row 41: purl.
Row 42: knit.

Back
Using No.4 needles and ecru, cast on 152/156/160 sts.
Row 1 (WS): *k2, p2, rep from * to end.
Row 2: *twist 2 (k into 2nd st on LH needle; don't slip it off needle, but knit into the first st and then slip both off the LH needle), p2, rep from * to end.
Keep repeating these 2 rows to form double twisted rib for 2½/3¼/3¼in, ending with a RS row. Purl the next row, inc into every 19th/19th/16th st (160/164/170 sts). Change to No. 5 needles and start working anchor panels from row 1, working 4/6/9 plain reverse st st sts at either end of the row and 8 sts between each panel (4 panels are worked across the row in all). When the 42 panel rows are worked, cont in rev st st for 4

more rows. Now work the wave pattern.
** Next row (RS): k0/2/5, *k2 tog, k7, inc into
the next 2 sts by knitting into the loop from
the previous row and then knitting into the
st itself. K7, k2 tog tbl, rep from * to last 0/2/5
sts, k to end.
Row 2: purl.
Repeat these 2 rows twice more.**
Work 4 rows in rev st st, then rep from ** to
**. Work 6 rows in st st.
Next row (RS): k5/7/10, k first row of Popeye
lettering chart, k10 sts in ecru, k "Popeye"
again, k to end in ecru. Cont working the
charts in st st in this position, until complete.
Work 6 rows in st st, then rep from ** to **.
Work 4 rows in rev st st, then rep from ** to
**. Work 6 rows in rev st st.
Next row (RS): p59/61/64, k first row of
Popeye face chart (right), p to end.
Cont working chart as established, with a
rev st st border on either side.
Row 9: p13/15/18, work first row of anchor
panel, p14, k chart sts, p14, work first row of
anchor panel, p to end.
Cont in pattern as established with 2 anchor
panels either side of Popeye. When the
anchor panels are complete, cont with chart
and rev st st border until chart is complete.
Work 4 rows in rev st st. Now work from **
to **. Work 4 rows in rev st st, then work
from ** to ** again. Work 6 rows in st st
followed by 16/16/20 rows in rev st st. Leave
sts on a spare needle.

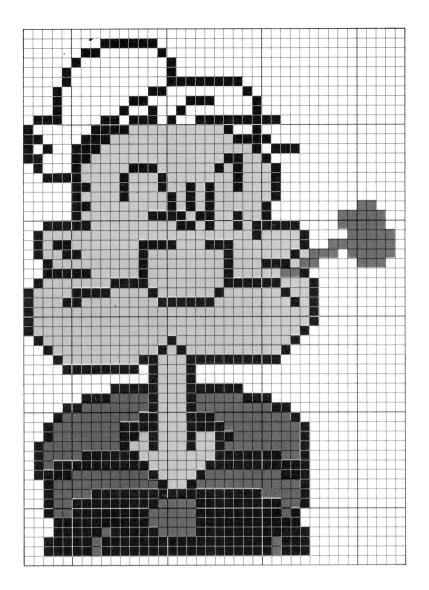

Front

Work as for back until 16/16/20 rows before
end. **Shape neck:** next (RS) row: p70/72/75,
bind off 20 sts purlwise, p to end. Cont with
this set of sts, in rev st st, leaving other sts
on a holder. Dec 1 st at neck edge on every
row until 55/57/60 sts remain. Work 0/0/4
rows even. Leave sts on a holder. Return to
other side of neck and shape to match.

Sleeves

Using No. 4 needles and ecru, cast on 50/54/
54 sts and work in double twisted rib for 2½/
2¾/3¼in, ending with a RS row.
Next row: p5/3/3, * inc into next st, p1, rep
from * to last 5/3/3 sts, p5/3/3 (70 sts). Change
to No. 5 needles.
Row 1: p19, work first row of anchor panel,
p to end. Cont working anchor panel in
pattern as established and inc 1 st at each
end of every 3rd row (working new sts in st
st or rev st st, as appropriate). When panel is
complete, work 4 rows in rev st st (100 sts

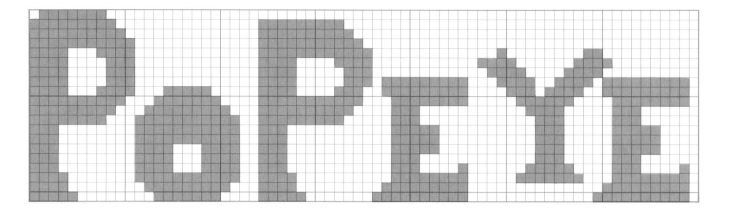

Incorporate this chart into the front and back of the guernsey, positioning it as described on page 43.

44

now on needle). Work wave pattern.

Next row: * k2 tog, k7, inc into next 2 sts as before, k7, k2 tog tbl, rep from * to end.

Row 2: purl.

Rep these last 2 rows twice more, keeping new sts in st st. Work 4 rows in rev st st, then work 6 wave rows again, keeping new sts in st st. Work 6 rows in st st.

Next row: k22, k first row of "Popeye" lettering chart, k to end. Cont working chart in this position until complete. Work 6 rows in st st (132 sts now on needle).

Next row: k6, *k2 tog, k7, inc into next 2 sts as before, k7, k2 tog, tbl, rep from * to last 6 sts, k6.

Row 2: purl.

Repeat last 2 rows twice more, working new sts in st st. Now work 4 rows in rev st st, then rep the 6 wave rows again, keeping new sts in st st. Now cont in rev st st, inc as before until you have 142/144/146 sts on the needle. Work 4 rows even, then bind off loosely.

Neckband

Knit LH shoulder seam tog with WS of work tog to form a ridge on RS of the work. Using No. 4 needles, ecru and with RS of work facing, knit up 50 sts along the back neck, 15/15/17 sts down left side, 20 sts across front and 15/15/17 sts up other side (100/100/104 sts). Work in double twisted rib for 2in, ending with a RS row. Bind off in ribbing.

Finishing

Knit second shoulder seam tog and join neckband edges with a flat seam. Open work out to lie flat and pin sleeves into place, slightly stretching them to avoid bunching. Attach with a flat seam. Join side and sleeve seams with a flat seam.

Kids' Character Jumpers

Materials
Melinda Coss worsted wool.
Popeye main color – contrast A – blue: 7/9/9/11oz; red (B): 3½oz; other colors from chart: less than 1¾oz of each.
Olive Oyl main color – contrast A – pink: 11/11/13/13oz; black (B): 6oz; other colors from chart: less than 1¾oz of each.
Betty Boop main color – contrast A – coral: 7/7/7/9oz; yellow (B): 3½oz; other colors from chart: less than 1¾oz of each.
2 buttons approximately ½in in diameter.

Needles
One pair of No. 3 and one pair of No. 5 needles.

Gauge
Using No. 5 needles and measured over st st, 26 sts and 30 rows = 4in square. Ribs worked on No. 3 needles.

The chart opposite (page 47) should be incorporated into the front of the Betty Boop version of the sweater, positioning it as shown on the chart on page 53.

A classic, slash-neck sweater with buttons on the shoulders and interchangeable motifs to fit kids aged 6,8,10 and 12 years.

Front
Using No. 3 needles and contrast B, cast on 91/97/103/109 sts. Work in k1, p1 rib for 2½in, ending with a WS row. Change to No. 5 needles and, using contrast A for background, begin following selected chart setting it up as follows: k2/5/8/11 sts. Work first row of chart, k to end.
Row 2: p2/5/8/11 sts, work 2nd row of chart, p to end. Cont working chart in this position until you have completed row 80/82/84/86.
Shape armholes: bind off 3 sts at beg of next 2 rows. Bind off 2 sts at beg of next 4 rows. Bind off 1 st at beg of next 6/8/10/12 rows (71/75/79/83 sts). Cont to work even until chart is complete. Work 20/29/38/47 rows. Change to contrast B and No. 3 needles and work 2 rows in k1, p1 rib. **Make buttonholes:** row 3: rib 3, bind off 2, rib 5/7/8/10, bind off 2, rib to end. Next row: cast on 2 sts over those bound off. Rib 2 more rows, bind off loosely in ribbing.

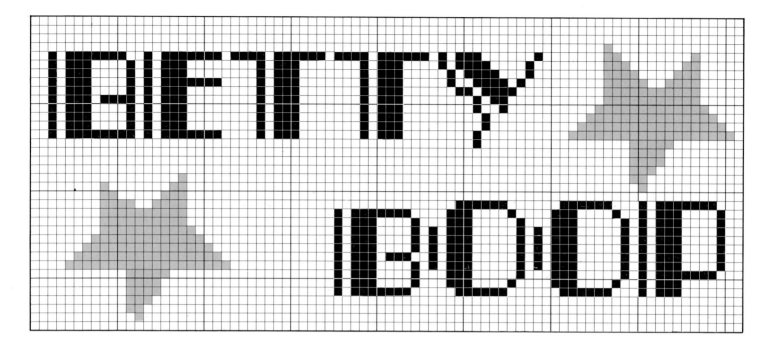

Incorporate this chart into the right sleeve of the Betty Boop sweater, positioning it as shown on the chart on page 54. The chart should be worked so that the letters run vertically up the sleeve.

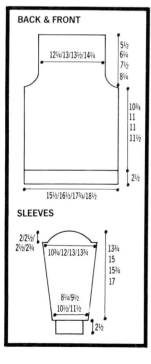

BACK & FRONT

12¼/13/13½/14¼

5½
6¼
7½
8¼

10¾
11
11
11½

2½

15½/16½/17¾/18½

SLEEVES

2/2½/
2½/2¾

10¾/12/13/13¾

13¾
15
15¾
17

8¼/9½
10½/11½

2½

Back
Work exactly as for front but omit chart.

Right sleeve
Using No. 3 needles and contrast B, cast on 40/44/48/52 sts. Work in k1, p1 rib for 2½in, inc 9/11/13/15 sts across last row of rib (49/55/61/67 sts). Change to No. 5 needles and main color and work in st st for 8 rows.

Row 9: begin reading selected chart and set up as follows: row 1: k5/8/11/14. K first row of chart, k to end. Cont working chart in this position, inc 1 st at each end of the next row and each following 10th/10th/12th/12th rows

50

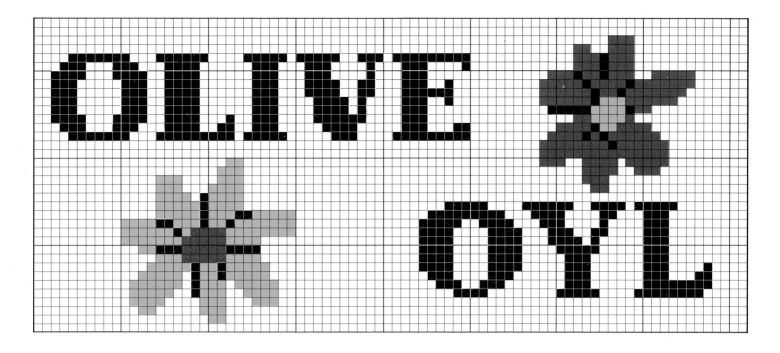

Incorporate the chart opposite (page 50) into the front of the Olive Oyl version, positioning it as shown on the chart on page 53. The chart above should be incorporated into the right sleeve, positioned as shown on page 54, with the letters running vertically up the sleeve.

6 times until you have 63/69/75/81 sts. Work even for 20/26/18/24 rows. **Shape sleeve cap:** bind off 3 sts at beg of the next 2 rows, 2 sts at beg of the next 4 rows, 1 st at beg of the next 16/18/18/20 rows, 2 sts at beg of the next 4/6/6/8 rows and 3 sts at beg of the next 4/4/6/6 rows. Bind off remaining 13 sts.

Left sleeve
Work as for right sleeve omitting chart.

Finishing
Lay front top ribbed border over back border. On the right side, sew borders together for 12/14/15/17 sts from the side. On the left side, overcast stitch border at short edges only. Position and sew buttons on left back shoulder to match buttonholes. Sew in sleeves using a narrow backstitch. Join side and sleeve seams with a flat seam.

The chart opposite (page 53) should be worked for the Popeye version of the sweater, while the chart on page 54 should be followed for the right sleeve.

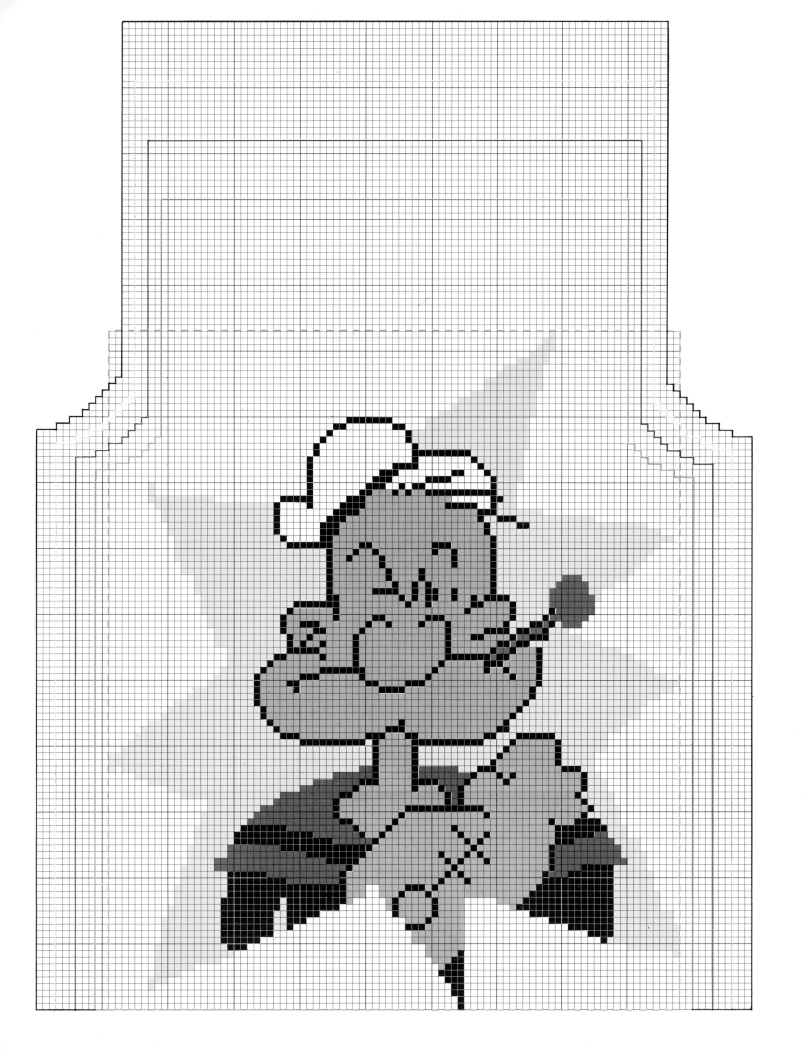

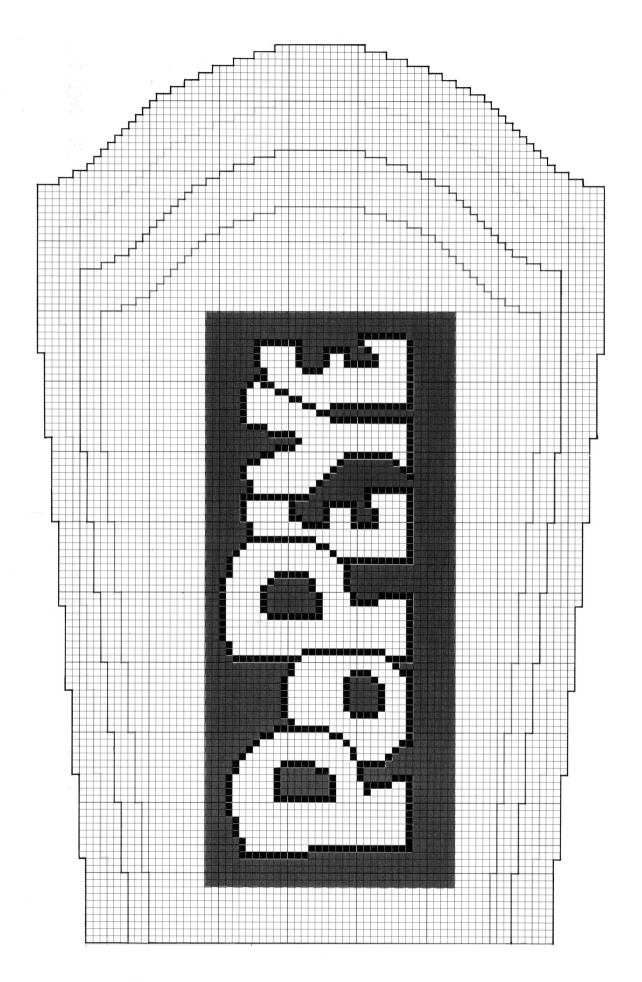

54

Olive Oyl in Spain

Seduced by the bright lights of Benidorm, the multi-talented Olive Oyl tries her skill at flamenco dancing. A frilly sweater dress in two sizes worked in stockinette stitch using the intarsia method (*see* Techniques, page 7).

Front

Using No. 3 needles and mauve, cast on 159/180 sts and work in garter st (knit every row) for ¾in. Change to No. 4 needles and mauve and begin following the chart on page 59 until it is complete. Next RS row: **form frill:**

Materials

Melinda Coss fingering weight wool – turquoise: 5oz; mauve: 5oz; all other colors to match chart: less than 1¾oz of each.

Needles

One pair of No. 3 and one pair of No. 4 needles.

Gauge

Using No. 4 needles and measured over st st, 28 sts and 36 rows = 4in square.

Follow the chart overleaf (page 56) to complete the front of the dress when the chart on page 59 has been worked.

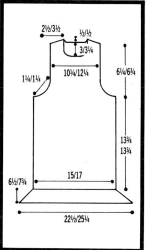

Work the chart opposite before you begin working the chart for the front and back of the dress. The chart should be knitted horizontally as it forms the frill at the hem of the dress.

*k1, k2 tog, rep from * to end (106/120 sts). Change to No. 3 needles and black and work in garter st for ¾in, ending with a RS row. Return to No. 4 needles and mauve, purl one row. ** Now begin working from the chart on page 56 in st st to armhole shaping. **Shape armholes:** bind off 6 sts at beg of the

next 2 rows, then dec 1 st at each end of every row until 74/88 sts remain. Work even to neck shaping. **Shape neck** (RS): k30/37, leave remaining sts on a spare needle. Working on this first set of sts only, dec 1 st at neck edge on every row until 22/29 sts remain. Now dec 1 st at neck edge on every

Follow the chart on page 57 to complete the back of the dress when the chart on page 59 has been worked.

alt row until 18/25 sts remain. Work even to shoulder shaping. **Shape shoulders:** bind off 6/8 sts at beg of the next 2 RS rows. Purl 1 row. Bind off. Rejoin yarn at neck edge to remaining sts. Bind off center 14 sts. K to end. Work shaping to match other side.

Back

Work as for front to **. Begin following chart for back to neck shaping, then work as follows. Work 20/27 sts. Slip remaining sts onto a spare needle. Working on this first set of sts only, dec 1 st at neck edge on next 2 rows (18/25 sts). Now shape shoulder as for front, working neck edge even. Rejoin yarn at neck edge. Bind off center 34 sts, work to end. Work shaping to match other side.

Neckband

Join left shoulder seam together using a narrow backstitch. Using No. 3 needles, main color and with RS facing, knit up 4 sts down right side of back, 34 sts across back, 4 sts up left back, 20 sts down left front, 14 sts across front and 20 sts up right front, (96 sts). Purl 1 row, then work in k1, p1 rib for 1in. Bind off in rib. Join the right shoulder seam with a narrow backstitch and the neckband edges with a flat seam.

Left armband

Using No. 3 needles, main color and with RS facing, begin at front armhole shaping and pick up 100 sts front to back. Purl 1 row, then work in k1, p1 rib for 1in. Bind off in ribbing.

Right armband

Work as for left armband but pick up from back to front.

Finishing

Join armband and body seams with a flat seam.

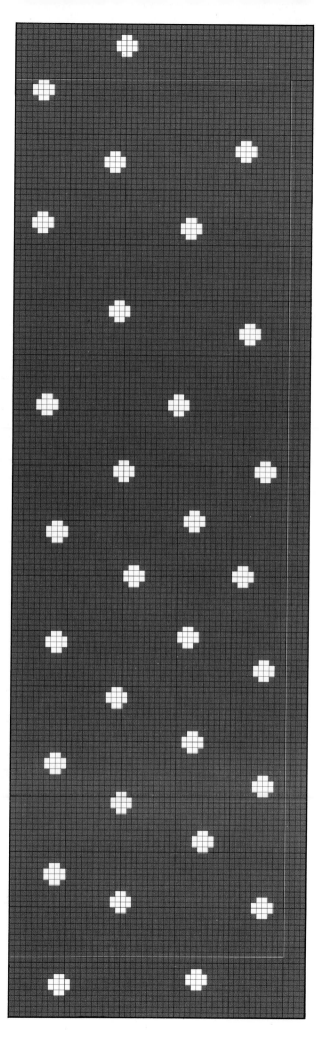

Betty Boop Mohair Jumper

Materials
Melinda Coss mohair –
fuchsia: 12oz; white: 7oz;
black: 1¾oz; all other
colors to match chart: less
than 1oz of each.

Needles
One pair of No. 7 and
one pair of No. 10
needles.

Gauge
Using No. 10 needles and
measured over st st, 16
sts and 16 rows = 4in
square. Ribs worked on
No. 7 needles.

Incorporate the chart
opposite (page 61) into the
front of the sweater,
positioning it as described on
page 63.

Betty Boop is one of the most enduring and
glamorous sex symbols of our time. Here she
is where she belongs – among the stars. This
oversized mohair sweater is worked using
the intarsia method (*see* Techniques, page 7).

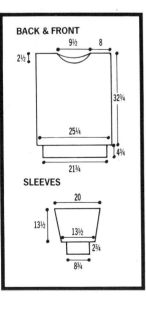

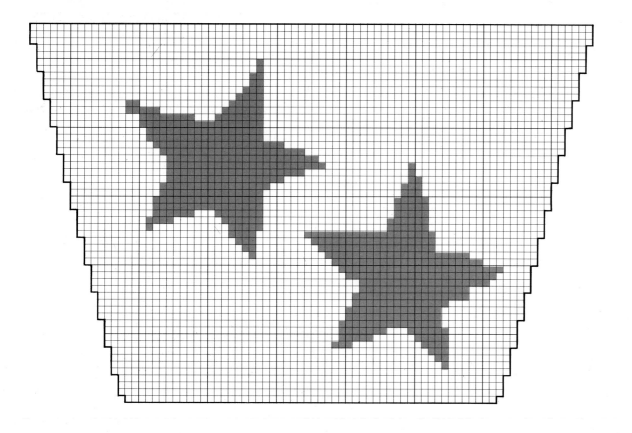

Back

Using No. 7 needles and white, cast on
88 sts. Work in k1, p1 rib for 4¾in, inc 14 sts
evenly across last row of rib. Change to
No. 10 needles and fuchsia and begin
following chart in st st to **neck shaping:** k34,
leave remaining sts on a spare needle and
work on this first set of sts only. Dec 1 st at
neck edge on next 2 rows. Leave remaining
32 sts on a holder. Rejoin yarn at neck edge,
bind off 34 sts, k to end. Repeat shaping as
for other side of neck.

Front

Work as for back, following the chart for
front to neck shaping. K39 sts. Leave
remaining sts on a spare needle. Working on
this first set of sts only, dec 1 st at neck edge
on every row until 32 sts remain. Work 1 row
even, leave sts on a spare needle. Rejoin
yarn at neck edge, bind off center 24 sts,
work to end of row. Work shaping to match
other side of neck.

Sleeves

Using No. 7 needles and fuchsia, cast on
36 sts and work in k1, p1 rib for 2¾in, inc
into every alt st on the last row of rib (54 sts).
Change to No. 10 needles and white and
begin following chart in st st, 1 st at each end
of the first row and every following 4th row
until you have 82 sts. Work 2 rows even and
bind off loosely.

Neckband

Knit the left shoulder seam together. Using
No. 7 needles and white and with RS facing,
k up 38 sts around the back neck, 7 sts down
left front, 24 sts across center front and 7 sts
up the other side of the neck (76 sts). Purl
1 row, bind off loosely.

Finishing

Knit the second shoulder seam together and
join neckband edges with a flat seam. Turn
the neckband to wrong side and slip st
bound-off edge to pick-up edge. Join sleeves
to body with a fine backstitch. Join side and
sleeve seams with a flat seam.

The chart opposite (page 62)
should be incorporated into
the back of the sweater. The
chart above should be
worked for the sleeves.

I Am a Rare Flower

Yes, we agree, Olive, and don't you look good in your flowery, drop-sleeved, crew-necked sweater in light-weight worsted wool, worked using the intarsia method (*see* Techniques, page 7).

Back
Using No. 4 needles and turquoise, cast on 104/112/120 sts. Work in k2, p2 rib for 3¼in, inc 21/17/13 sts evenly across last row of rib (125/129/133 sts). Change to No. 6 needles

Materials
Melinda Coss light-weight worsted wool – turquoise: 18oz; red, white, black, gold, flesh and tan: less than 1¾oz of each.

Needles
One pair of No. 4 and one pair of No. 6 needles; one 16in circular needle.

Gauge
Using No. 6 needles and measured over st st, 24 sts and 30 rows = 4in square. Ribs worked on No. 4 needles.

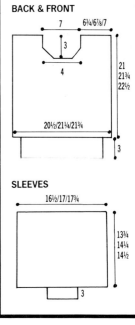

BACK & FRONT

SLEEVES

The entire chart should be worked for the front of the sweater. The three flowers at the bottom left of the chart should be incorporated into the back of the sweater, but positioned as shown on the chart and described on page 68. The single flower at the bottom right of the chart should be incorporated into both sleeves, positioned as described on page 68.

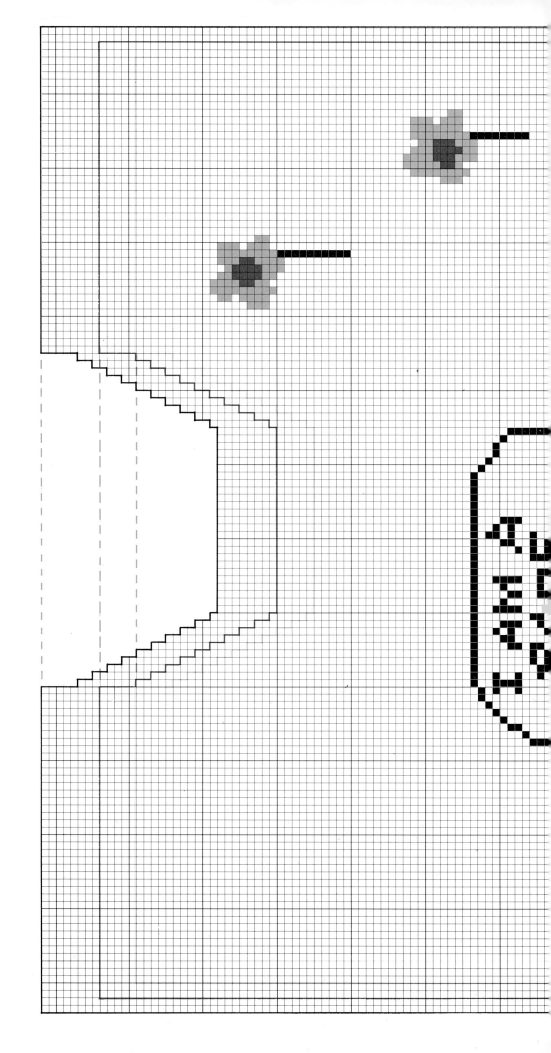

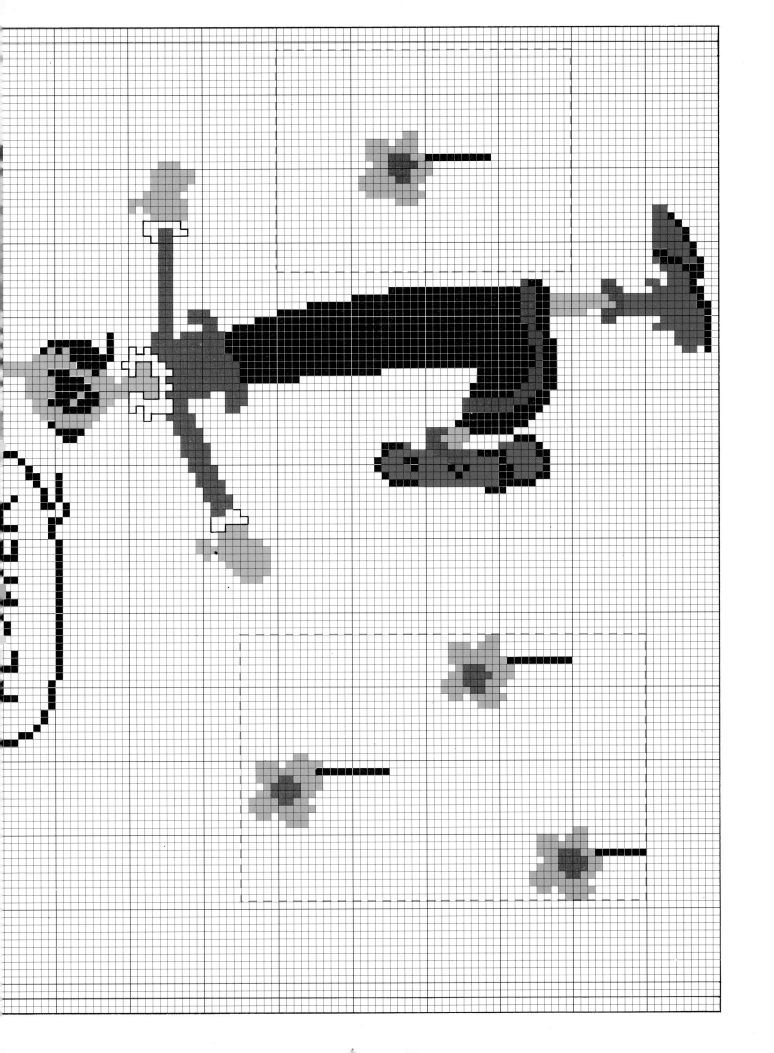

and begin following chart * working *only* the three flowers shown in the box and keeping them in position as indicated. Cont in turquoise only, until the whole chart is complete. Leave sts on a spare needle.

Front
Work as for back to *, cont following chart for front until 136/142/148 rows have been worked.

Shape neck: next row: work 50/52/54 sts, slip these sts onto a spare needle, bind off center 25 sts and work to end. Cont on this last set of sts only, dec 1 st at neck edge on the next and every following alt row until 40/42/44 sts remain. Work even until front matches back in length. Leave remaining 40/42/44 sts on a spare needle. Work shaping to match other side of neck.

Shoulder seams
Place front and back pieces RS tog and knit tog first 40/42/44 sts from the back with the front shoulder seam. Repeat for second shoulder seam, leaving remaining center back sts on a holder.

Pocket linings (Make 2)
Using No. 6 needles and turquoise, cast on 30 sts and work 40 rows in st st. Leave sts on a spare needle.

Sleeves
Using No. 4 needles and turquoise, cast on 52/52/56 sts. Work in k2, p2 rib for 2¾in, inc 49/51/53 sts evenly across last row of rib (101/103/109 sts). Change to No. 6 needles and begin working in st st until you have completed 24 rows. Begin following chart for sleeve, setting up pattern as follows: k35/37/39 sts. K first row of chart, k35/37/39 sts to end. Cont working chart in this position until it is complete. **Pocket row:** work 35/37/39 sts, slip center 30 sts onto a holder, work to end. Next row: work back to slipped sts and replace these with a pocket lining, work to end. Cont working even until 106/108/110 rows have been worked. Bind off loosely.

Pocket trims
Using No. 4 needles and turquoise, pick up the 30 sts held for top of pocket and work in k2, p2 rib for 4 rows. Bind off. Sew pocket linings in place and sew down side edges of pocket trim.

Neckband
Using a 16in circular needle and with RS of work facing, pick up and knit 25 sts down left side of neck, 25 sts from center front, 25 sts up right side of neck and 45 sts held for back of neck (120 sts). Work in k2, p2 rib for 2in. Bind off loosely in ribbing.

Finishing
Join sleeves to body using a narrow backstitch. Join side and sleeve seams using a flat seam.

Oh, Popeye!

Popeye, our one-eyed, spinach-eating sailor, is an all-American hero, but his most adoring fan is Olive Oyl who frequently and loudly declares her love. A sporty worsted-weight cotton jacket with pockets and a fly front that is worked using the intarsia method (*see* Techniques, page 7).

Back

Using No. 4 needles and green, cast on 92 sts.
Row 1: p2, *k4, p2, rep from * to end.
Row 2: k2, *p4, k2, rep from * to end.
Repeat the last 2 rows 11 times more, inc 8 sts evenly across the last row of rib (100 sts). Change to No. 6 needles and begin following the chart in st st, starting with a k row. *At the same time*, inc 1 st at each end of the 2nd and every following 3rd rows until you have 130 sts. **Shape raglans:** bind off 6 sts at beg of the next 2 rows. Dec 1 st at each end of every following alt row until 30 sts remain. Work 3 rows even. Bind off.

Left front

Using No. 4 needles and green, cast on 64 sts.
Row 1: p2, *k4, p2, rep from * to last 20 sts, k20.
Row 2: k3 (these first three sts are k on *every*

Materials
Melinda Coss worsted-weight cotton – apple green: 18oz; black: 3½oz; white: 7oz; all other colors to match chart: less than 1¾oz of each.
7 buttons approximately 1in in diameter.

Needles
One pair of No. 4 and one pair of No. 6 needles.

Gauge
Using No. 6 needles and measured over st st, 20 sts and 24 rows = 4in square. Ribs worked on No. 4 needles.

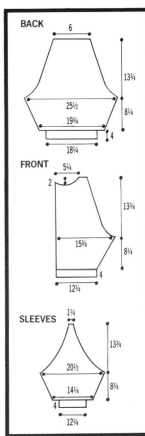

BACK
6
13¾
25½
8¼
19¾
4
18¼

FRONT
5¼
2
13¾
15¾
8¼
4
12¾

SLEEVES
1¼
13¾
20½
8¾
14¼
4
12¼

This chart should be used to complete the right front of the jacket. The dotted line indicates the position of the pocket welt.

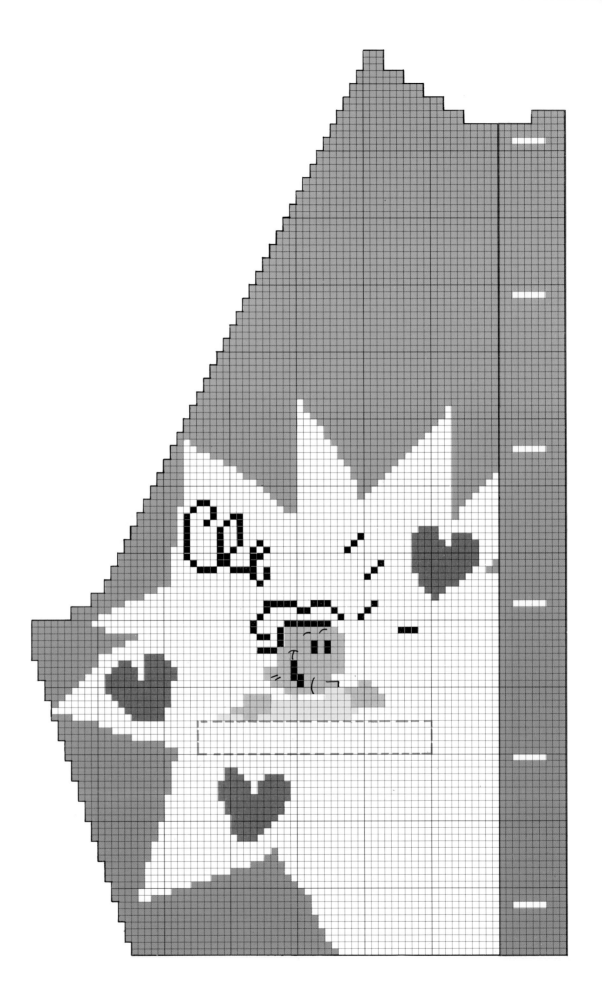

70

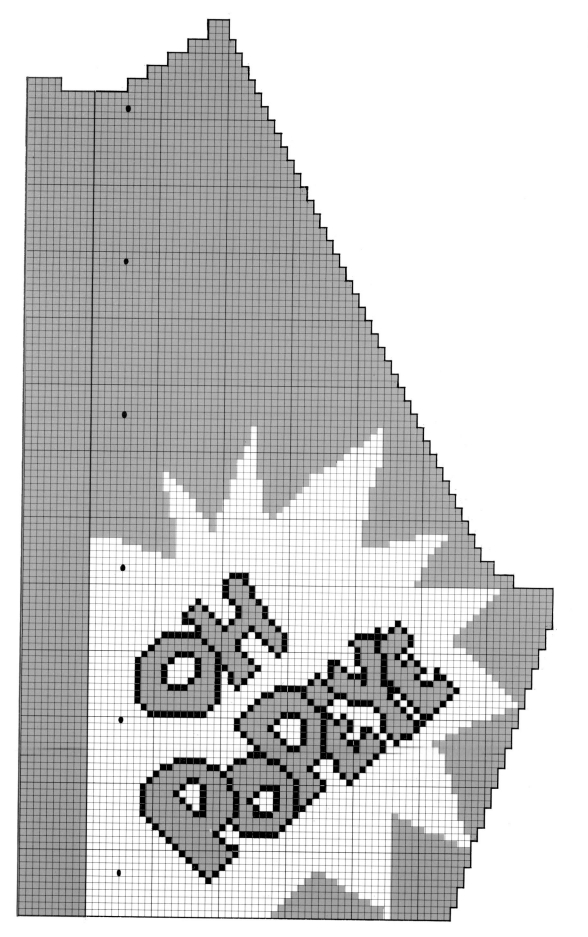

This chart should be used to complete the left front of the jacket.

Follow this chart for the back
of the jacket.

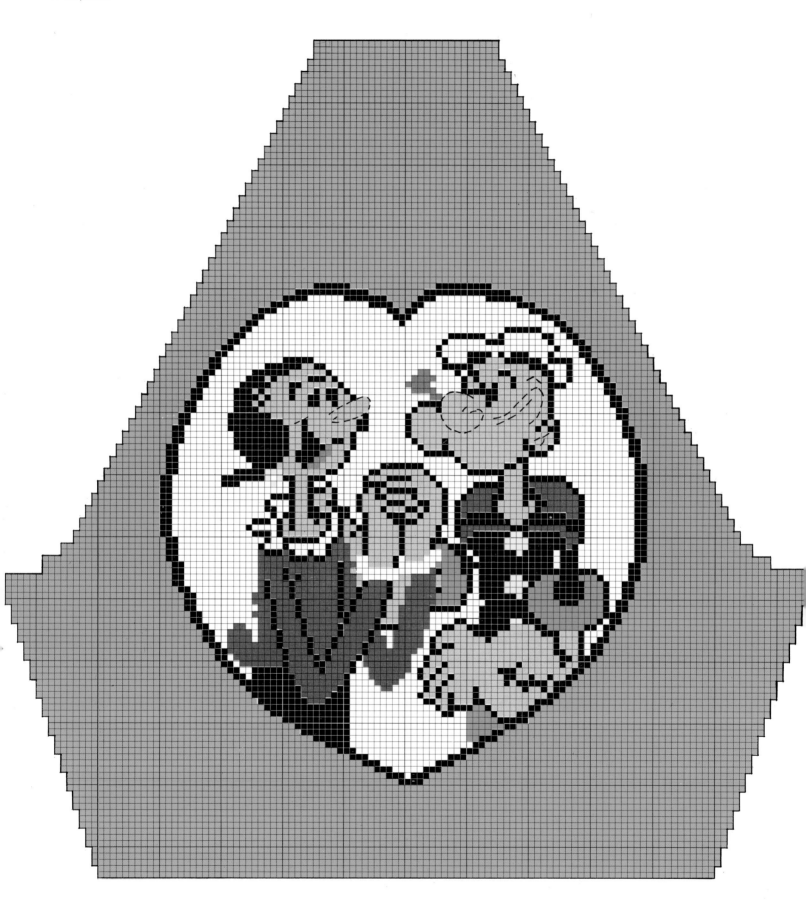

72

Incorporate this chart into the left sleeve only. The right sleeve is worked in the stripe sequence.

row up to the neck-shaping). P17, k2, *p4, k2, rep from * to end. Repeat these last 2 rows 11 times more. Inc 1 st on last row of rib. Change to No. 6 needles and begin following chart in st st, starting with a k row for 30 rows. *At the same time* inc 1 st at the right-hand edge of the 2nd row and every following 3rd row until you have 80 sts. Work 5 rows even. Next row (RS): **shape raglan**: bind off 6 sts at beg of this row, 3 sts at beg of the following alt row, then 1 st at beg of every alt row until you have 34 sts. **Shape neck** (RS): k19, bind off 10 sts, k to end. Next row, k5, turn, bind off. Rejoin yarn to remaining sts and bind off 3 sts at neck edge of every alt row until 3 sts remain. *At the same time*, work raglan shaping as established. Work 2 rows even on remaining 3 sts. Bind off.

Pocket lining

Using No. 6 needles and white, cast on 35 sts. Work in st st for 30 rows. Leave sts on a spare needle.

Right front

Using No. 4 needles and green, cast on 64 sts.
Row 1: k20, p2, *k4, p2, rep from * to end.
Row 2: k2, *p4, k2, rep from * to last 20 sts, p17, k3. Repeat these 2 rows 11 times more. *At the same time*, after the 6th rib row (ending on a WS), work first buttonhole as follows: k3, bind off 5 sts, work rib row to end. Cast on 5 sts over buttonhole on next row. Complete rib, inc 1 st on last row. Change to No. 6 needles and start following the chart for right front, working in st st until 30 rows are complete. **Make pocket opening**: next row (RS): k20, slip 35 sts onto a holder, rejoin yarn, k to end. On return row, keeping shaping as established, p across sts held for pocket in place of those bound off. Work as for left front, reversing shapings, and make buttonholes as described every 24 rows (7 in all).

Left sleeve

Using No. 4 needles and green, cast on 62 sts. Work rib as for back inc 10 sts evenly across last row of rib (72 sts). Change to No. 6 needles and begin following chart, in st st, starting with a k row. Inc 1 st at each end of the 2nd row and every following 3rd row until you have 106 sts. Work 1 row even. **Shape raglan**: bind off 6 sts at beg of next 2 rows, 3 sts at beg of next 2 rows and 2 sts at beg of the following 2 rows. Then dec 1 st at each end of every following alt row until you have 6 sts. Work 2 rows even, then bind off.

Right sleeve

Work as for left sleeve but in stripe sequence only – i.e., ignore heart and "LUV" motif.

Collar

Join shoulder seams. Fold back the first 9 sts of each front, center front. Using No. 4 needles and green, pick up and k 22 sts up right front (working through 2 sts on fold), 4 sts on sleeve top, 28 sts across the back, 4 sts across the sleeve top, 22 sts down left front (working last 9 sts through 2 sts). Work 4in in garter st (knit every row) and *at the same time* on every 4th row, k4, inc 1, k to last 4 sts, inc 1, k4. Cont to inc in this manner on every 4th row until you have 90 sts. Bind off.

Finishing

Stitch down folds using slip st. Set in sleeves and join side and sleeve seams. Sew on buttons to match buttonholes.

Pocket trim

Using No. 4 needles and white, pick up 35 sts held for pocket trim. K1, p1 rib for 3 rows. Bind off. Stitch pocket in place, stitch down edges of trim.

Hägar the Horrible Sweater

Materials
Melinda Coss heavy-weight worsted sport –
grey tweed: 18oz;
turquoise tweed: 11oz;
lilac tweed: 1¾oz; plain
black: 3½oz; plain white,
pale blue, slate, royal
blue, orange, flesh, red
and gold: less than 1¾oz
of each.

Needles
One pair of No. 4 and
one pair of No. 7 needles;
one 16in circular needle.

Gauge
Using No. 7 needles and
measured over st st, 18 sts
and 25 rows = 4in square.
Ribs worked on No. 4
needles.

Follow the chart opposite
(page 77) for the front of the
sweater and the chart on
page 78 for the back.

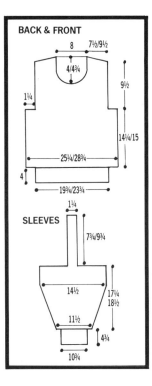

As Helga calls in vain, the mighty warrior
Hägar crosses mountains to reach her. A
tweedy, heavy-weight worsted sweater in
two sizes worked using the intarsia method
(*see* Techniques, page 7).

Back
Using No. 4 needles and grey tweed, cast on
90/108 sts. Work in k1, p1 rib for 25 rows, inc
26/24 sts evenly across last row of rib (116/132
sts). Change to No. 7 needles and begin

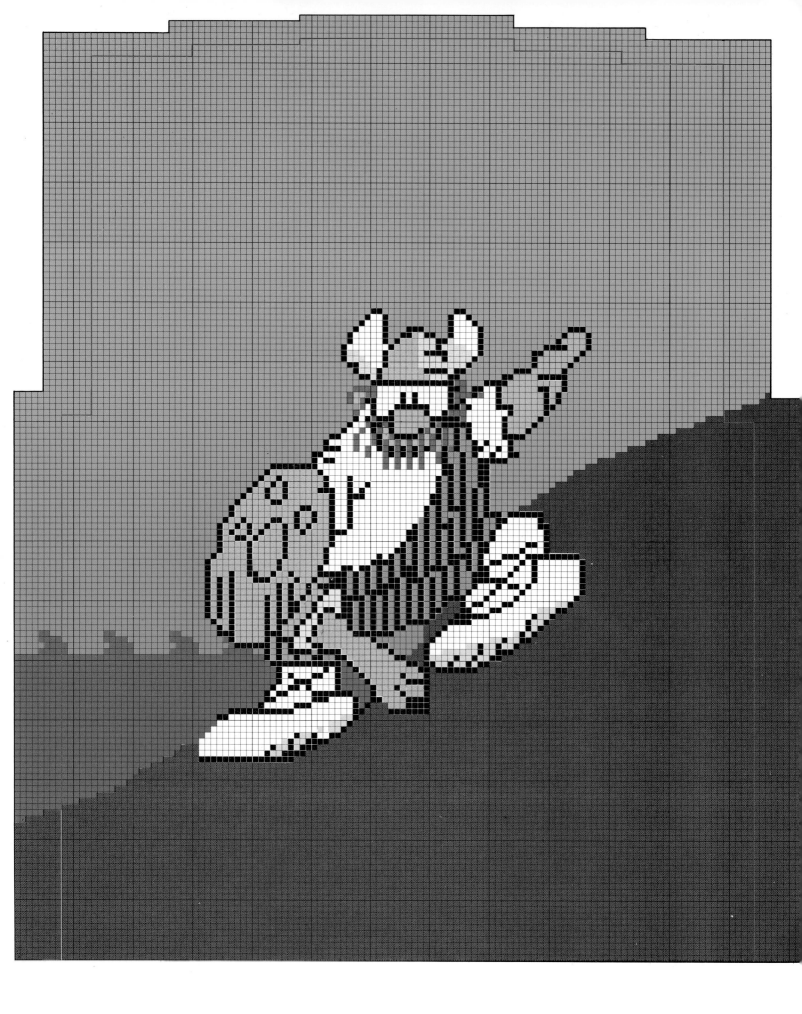

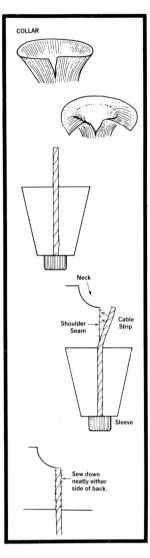

following chart in st st until 90/94 rows have been worked. **Shape armholes:** bind off 5 sts at beg of next 2 rows. Work 60 rows even. *
Shape shoulders: bind off 17/21 sts at beg of next 2 rows. Bind off 18/22 sts at beg of the following 2 rows. Bind off remaining 36/36 sts.

Front

Work as for back to *. Cont to work even until 128/132 rows of the chart have been worked. **Shape neck:** next row: k47/55 sts. Work on these sts only, leaving the remaining sts on a spare needle. Bind off 4 sts at beg of the next row, 3 sts at beg of the following row, 2 sts at beg of the next 2 alt rows and 1 st at neck edge on the following 7th row (35/43 sts). Work even until front matches back to shoulder shaping, ending on a WS row. Bind off remaining 17/21 sts at beg of the next row. Work 1 row even, bind off 18/22 sts. With RS facing, rejoin yarn to remaining sts. Bind off center 12 sts. Work one row even. Complete shaping as for other side of neck.

Sleeves

Using No. 4 needles and grey tweed, cast on 48 sts. Work in k1, p1 rib for 30 rows, inc 4 sts evenly across last row of rib (52 sts). Change to No. 7 needles and begin working in st st working a central cabled stripe as follows:
Row 1: k22 in grey, k8 in lilac, k22 in grey.
Row 2: p22 in grey, p8 in lilac, p22 in grey.

Repeat these 2 rows, inc 1 st at each end of the 4th row and every following 4th row until you have 92 sts. *At the same time,* when 8 rows of st st have been worked, make a cable as follows: inc 1, k23 in grey, slip next 4 sts onto a cn and hold at front of work. K4 in lilac, k4 from cn in lilac, k23 in grey. Repeat striped cable in this way on every 8th row. When you have completed your shaping, work even on the 92 sts until sleeve measures 22/23¼in from the beg. Bind off 42 sts, hold center 8 sts on a spare needle, bind off 42 sts. Cont working striped cable only for another 7¾/9¾in (or until cable band reaches the length of the shoulder seam). Bind off.

Finishing

Join right shoulder seam using a flat seam. Stitch right sleeve to body, sewing cable band down neatly on both edges so that it covers the shoulder seam.
Repeat for left shoulder and sleeve.

Collar

Using a 16in circular needle and with RS of work facing, k up 32 sts down left side of neck, 12 sts from center front, 32 sts from right side of neck and 36 sts across back neck (112 sts). Work in k1, p1 rib for 4 rows, ending at center front. **Make collar opening:** turn, rib back to center front, turn, rib back to center front. Cont working in this way for 20 rows more. Bind off in ribbing.
Join side and sleeve seams using a flat seam.

Et Tu Brutus?

Brutus has a huge body and a tiny brain. No matter how many times he is knocked out he still believes he can defeat Popeye and win Olive's love. This bulky macho sweater featuring Brutus plotting his way into Olive's heart is worked using the intarsia method (*see* Techniques, page 7).

Front

Using No. 10 needles and green, cast on 82 sts and work in k1, p1 rib for 10 rows, inc 6 sts evenly across last row of rib (88 sts). ** Change to No. 10½ needles and work in st st, following the chart until 114 rows have been completed. **Shape neck:** k35, leave

Materials

Melinda Coss bulky-weight wool – grass green: 23oz; aqua: 23oz; gold: 3½oz; taupe: 3½oz; black, silver, flesh, orange, white and royal blue: 1¾oz of each.

Needles

One pair of No. 10 and one pair of No. 10½ needles.

Gauge

Using No. 10½ needles and measured over st st, 13 sts and 16 rows = 4in square. Ribs worked on No. 10 needles.

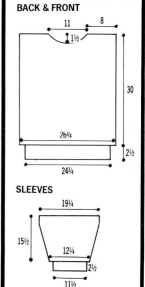

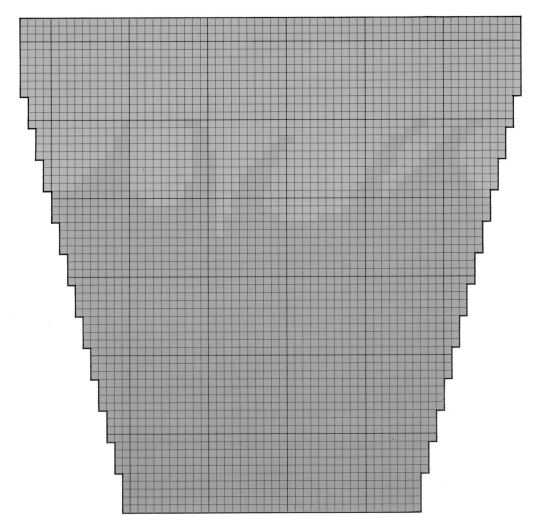

Work the chart opposite (page 82) for the front of the sweater, knitting all of the motif. To complete the back of the sweater, knit the bottom half of the chart (up to the red line) in green, changing to blue to complete the top half. The chart (left) should be followed for both sleeves.

center 18 sts on a spare needle, k to end. Working each side of the neck separately, bind off 3 sts at neck edge on next row, 1 st on the following row, 3 sts on the next row and 1 st on the two following rows. Work 1 row, leave remaining 26 sts on a holder.

Back

Work as for front to **. Follow the chart for the front of the sweater, working the bottom half in green only to where the red line indicates. Change to blue and work the top half of the back in blue only. When back matches front to shoulder shaping, leave sts on a spare needle, placing a marker 26 sts in on both sides.

Sleeves

Using No. 10 needles, cast on 36 sts in green and work in k1, p1 rib for 10 rows, inc 1 st at each end of last row of rib (38 sts). Follow the sleeve chart, inc 1 st at each end of the 5th row and every following 4th row until you have 64 sts. Work even in aqua only until sleeve measures 18in. Bind off loosely.

Neckband

Knit right shoulder seams together. Using No. 10 needles, aqua and with RS facing, pick up and k 10 sts across left front, 18 sts held for center front, 10 sts up right front and 36 sts between markers on center back (74 sts). Work in k1, p1 rib for 15 rows. Bind off in ribbing.

Finishing

Knit left shoulder seams together. Join sleeves to sweater. Join side and sleeve seams using flat seams. Fold neckband to wrong side and slip stitch bound-off edge to pick-up edge.

The Phantom

Materials
Melinda Coss light-weight
worsted wool – black:
18oz; red: 7oz; white:
3½oz; gold: 3½oz; all
other contrast colors to
match chart: less than 1oz
of each.

Needles
One pair of No. 4 needles
and one pair of No. 5
needles.

Gauge
Using No. 5 needles and
measured over st st, 24
sts and 30 rows = 4in
square. Ribs worked on
No. 4 needles.

Follow the chart opposite
(page 85) to complete the
front of the sweater.

Defender of justice with strange,
extraordinary powers, The Phantom uses
secrets taught to him by the natives of the
Deep Woods and draws on the strength of
jungle tigers. This man-sized light-weight
worsted sweater is worked in stockinette
stitch using the intarsia method (*see*
Techniques, page 7).

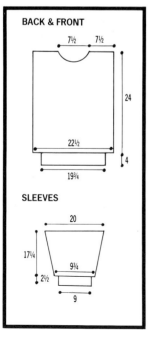

BACK & FRONT

SLEEVES

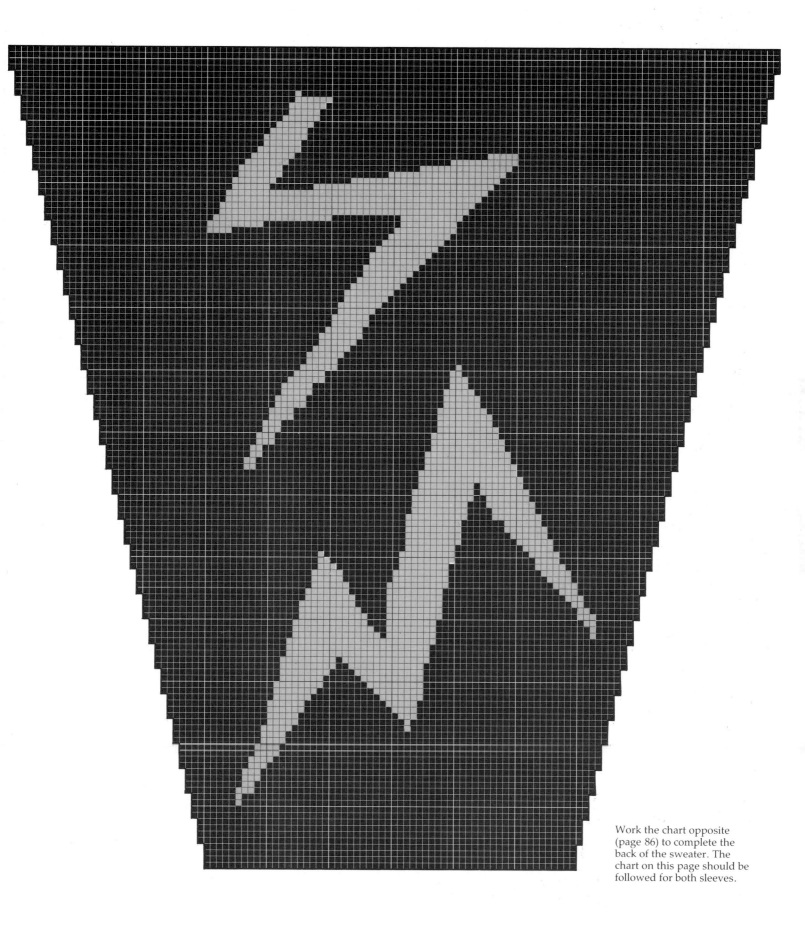

Work the chart opposite
(page 86) to complete the
back of the sweater. The
chart on this page should be
followed for both sleeves.

Front

Using No. 4 needles and black, cast on 120 sts. Work in k1, p1 rib for 4in, inc 18 sts evenly across the last row of rib (138 sts). Change to No. 5 needles and red and work in st st * following the chart until you reach the neck shaping.

Shape neck: k56, slip the remaining sts onto a spare needle and, working on this first set of sts only, dec 1 st at neck edge on the next row and the following 10 alt rows. Work 8 rows even, slip remaining 45 sts onto a stitch holder. Rejoin yarn at inner edge to held sts. Bind off center 26 sts. K to end, work shaping to match other side of neck.

Back

Work as for front to *. Cont following the chart for the back until you reach the shoulder. Place a marker 45 sts in on each end to mark the shoulder shaping. Hold sts on a spare needle.

Sleeves

Using No. 4 needles and black, cast on 56 sts. Work in k1, p1 rib for 2½in inc 4 sts evenly across last row of rib (60 sts). Change to No. 5 needles and cont in black, following the chart in st st, inc 1 st at each end of every 4th row until you have 124 sts. Work even until the sleeve chart is complete. Bind off loosely.

Neckband

Knit one shoulder seam together. Using No. 4 needles and black, pick up and knit the 48 sts held for center back, 30 sts down one side of front, 26 sts held for center front and 30 sts up second side of front (134 sts). Work in k1, p1 rib for 2½in. Bind off.

Finishing

Knit second shoulder seam together. Turn neckband to wrong side and slip st bound-off edge to pick-up edge. Sew sleeves to sweater and join sleeve and body seams using a flat seam.

Ming the Merciless

Materials
Melinda Coss 8-ply DK
mercerized cotton – khaki:
23oz; red: 3½oz; black,
orange, yellow: 3½oz of
each; all other colors to
match chart: less than
1¾oz of each.

Needles
One pair of No. 4 needles
and one pair of No. 5
needles.

Gauge
Using No. 5 needles and
measured over st st, 24 sts
and 30 rows = 4in square.
Ribs worked on No. 4
needles.

This sweater is worked in
the same basic pattern as
The Phantom (*see*
previous pattern), except
that the front and back
(including bands) are
worked in khaki through-
out. The sleeves are
worked in khaki only.

An evil tyrant from the dying planet Mongo,
Ming the Merciless has sworn to seize and
dominate the Earth. A companion to The
Phantom, this light-weight sweater is
worked in double-knitting mercerized cotton
using the intarsia method (*see* Techniques,
page 7).

The chart opposite (page 91)
should be followed for the
front of the sweater, and the
chart on page 92 should be
worked to complete the back.
The sleeves of this sweater
are plain, but follow the
instructions for The Phantom
sweater on page 89.

Abbreviations

alt	alternate	m1	make one – i.e., inc 1 st by working the st below the next st to be worked into on the left-hand needle, then into the st itself
BC	back cross – slip next st onto a cable needle and hold at back of work, k1, then p1 from cable needle		
beg	begin(ning)	p	purl
cf	cable front	p-b	purl into back of st
cn	cable needle	psso	pass slipped stitch over
cont	continue/continuing	rep	repeat
dec	decrease/decreasing	rev st st	reverse st st
dpn	double pointed needle	RH	right hand
FC	front cross – slip next st onto a cable needle and hold at front of work, p1, then k1 from cable needle	RS	right side
		sktpo	slip next st, k2 tog, pass slipped st over
		sl	slip
in	inch(es)	ssk	slip 1, knit 1, pass slipped stitch over
inc	increase/increasing		
k	knit	st(s)	stitch(es)
k-b	knit into back of st	st st	stockinette stitch
LH	left hand	tbl	through back of loop(s)
MB	make bobble	tog	together
		WS	wrong side

Yarn Information

All the sample garments illustrated in this book were knitted in Yarnworks yarns. For a list of Yarnworks stockists plus full information on the mail order service and price list, contact Marcus Corps, 117 Dobbins Street, Brooklyn 11222, New York, or telephone 718 383 7321.

For those who wish to substitute different yarns, weights are given throughout to the nearest 1oz ball. A 1oz ball of 4-ply cotton is approximately 92 yards, of 6-ply cotton, approximately 62 yards, and of 8-ply cotton, approximately 46 yards; a 1oz bale of slub cotton is approximately 78 yards. To obtain the best results you must ensure that the gauge recommended on your selected yarn *matches the gauge* printed in our patterns. We cannot guarantee your results if this rule is not followed.